ONE GOAL

TRIUMPH
BOOKS

Rising stars such as Jonathan Toews (far left) and Patrick Kane (far right) have reenergized Blackhawks fans.

Coca-Cola®

This book is available in quantity at special discounts for your group
or organization. For further information, contact:

Triumph Books
542 South Dearborn Street
Suite 750
Chicago, Illinois 60605
(312) 939-3330
Fax (312) 663-3557

Printed in United States of America
ISBN: 978-1-60078-249-7

Photos courtesy of Chicago Blackhawks except where otherwise indicated

Content packaged by Mojo Media, Inc.
Joe Funk: Editor
Jason Hinman: Creative Director

Chicago Blackhawks Staff
Jay Blunk: Senior Vice President of Business Operations
Adam Kempenaar: Director of New Media and Publications
John Sandberg: New Media and Publications Assistant
Brad Boron: Contributing Writer
Amanda Dennin: New Media and Publications Intern

contents

Patrick Kane holds the Calder Memorial Trophy after being named the league's top rookie at the NHL Awards Ceremony on June 12, 2008.

Foreword by Bobby Hull

If you aren't proud of your past, you sure as hell aren't going anywhere in your future. For a long time both the Blackhawks and I tried to forget about our pasts.

Thirty-five long years went by between the day I left for Winnipeg and the day Blackhawks President John McDonough called offering me a chance to once again join the franchise that I loved so fiercely. I honestly never thought I'd be allowed back into the fold.

During my time away from the Blackhawks family, there was a void in my life. When it was over in Winnipeg, I was left without a home. Through all of that, a lot of people wouldn't let me forget that I was a Blackhawk. Now I no longer have to try.

Just as I was re-embraced by the team, the city of Chicago has once again embraced the glory of Blackhawks hockey. Rocky Wirtz and John McDonough have dipped into the past and brought out the dominant players of the 1950s, '60s, and '70s as ambassadors, and I see players on the team now that parallel our rise in the late '50s, when a guy nicknamed "Mikita the Magician" and yours truly would go on to lead the Hawks to their last Stanley Cup in 1961.

It means so much to me to say that I'm a Blackhawk again, and it means even more to see the legions of fans supporting the team the way they did back when Stan and I laced up the skates. Things are looking bright for the future, and Rocky and John are ready to take the team to the same heights we reached during those great years.

I believe that this team is going to take the same course we did, coming out of the basement and going all the way to win a championship. I can't imagine what will go on in Chicago when the Blackhawks win their next Stanley Cup. I hope I'm around to witness the tremendous enjoyment the city will get.

It will be a thing to remember. ●

Bobby Hull, one of the top scorers in NHL history, played for the Chicago Blackhawks from 1957 to 1972. "The Golden Jet" still holds the Hawks' record for career goals (604).

Bobby Hull, along with Stan Mikita, was named a
Blackhawks Ambassador in a pregame ceremony
on March 7, 2008.

STAN MIKITA

Foreword by Pat Foley

Even looking in from the outside, I could clearly see that the Chicago Blackhawks were changing. From the minute Rocky Wirtz took over, I knew something great was happening. Televising home games...welcoming back all-time greats Bobby Hull, Stan Mikita and Tony Esposito...acquiring marquee talent...stating definitively that the goal here is to win the Stanley Cup...there was a culture change happening on Madison Street. Long-suffering Hawks fans—and if there was a stronger way to say "long-suffering," I would say it—were finally getting the kind of treatment that should have come to them a long time ago.

A young, talented Blackhawks team is now taking the ice. There will be some painful lessons along the way, but they've got enough skill and character to overcome those tough times. Watching kids such as Patrick Kane and Jonathan Toews gets me excited for the future of hockey in Chicago. If they improve as they should, it will be a lot of fun to come to the rink every night.

Rocky, John McDonough, and company have awakened a sleeping giant in Chicago. Fans of Blackhawks hockey who were just waiting for something, anything, to hang their hats on are back and filling the United Center with the type of energy and enthusiasm that can impact the game on the ice. They've been dying for something to be excited about, and they finally have it.

I've seen what it can be like in this city when you have a really good team, a team that's a legitimate contender in Chicago...there's nothing like it.

Blackhawks history is written with commas, not periods, and this Hawks franchise is now constantly growing and maturing. If the team can continue to progress as I and Hawks fans everywhere believe it can, the Blackhawks have the personnel in place to become the premier franchise in the National Hockey League.

My goodness, that will be a beautiful thing. ●

Broadcaster Pat Foley, who served as the Hawks' play-by-play announcer from 1981 until 2006, is welcomed back to the booth at a July 2008 press conference. The 2008–09 season marks the first time in the franchise's history that all 82 regular-season games are being broadcast on television.

Blackhawks are Back!

New management, innovative approach excites fan base • By Ed Sherman

One game doesn't make a season, but one game did provide a microcosm of just how far the Blackhawks have come as an organization.

It all was wrapped up in a tidy package when the Hawks hosted the Detroit Red Wings on October 25. Just consider: hockey barely moves the needle in October, but on a Saturday night that featured the third game of the World Series, terrific college football match-ups, and Halloween festivities in full scare, a crowd of 22,690 fans jammed the United Center, setting the record for the largest regular-season crowd.

Prior to the game, the Hawks unveiled the special jerseys they will wear for their January 1 game against Detroit in Wrigley Field. The Winter Classic is the hottest ticket in town, the first time that's happened for the Blackhawks since the Bobby Hull era.

Speaking of Hull, he had previously been a distant legend, estranged from the team for years. But on this October night, he was back in the fold and positively beaming while modeling the Classic jersey for the cameras.

The entire scene was captured on WGN television and radio. Both powerhouse outlets carried the game in relationships that have been resumed with the Hawks for the first time since the 1970s.

On the TV call was Pat Foley, a long-time Hawks fixture who was back at his familiar post after two years in exile. Foley was in full throat as the young, vibrant Hawks took a 4–2 lead after two periods over their bitterest rival and the defending Stanley Cup champions.

With the United Center shaking, Blackhawks Chairman Rocky Wirtz had to marvel at how it all had come together so fast, so soon. "Yes, it's been surprising," Wirtz said.

General manager Dale Tallon, who has been with the Hawks for 30 years, admitted that he has been surprised, too. Then he added tellingly, "But the more you get know Rocky and [team president John McDonough], you're not surprised."

It all starts with Wirtz. W. Rockwell Wirtz—"Rocky," as he is more commonly known—took over the franchise on October 5, 2007. Wirtz inherited quite a task. The Hawks were in disarray, playing to small crowds in a town that barely acknowledged their existence. The team that once shined the brightest in the Chicago sports landscape had fallen off the map.

"I knew people were angry," Wirtz said. "But like John says, you worry when the fans go from anger to indifference. Then they don't care. I knew we had missed a couple of generations of hockey fans."

Wirtz acted quickly to change the culture from inside and out. His first public move was a stunner. For years, Wirtz's father, Bill, had resisted intense public pressure to air home games on local television. It had become a lightning-rod issue that defined a franchise that seemed to have lost its way.

Imagine the surprise Jim Corno, the president of Comcast Sports Net, had when Wirtz, barely settled into the new job, approached him about airing Hawks home games.

Rookie of the Year Patrick Kane addresses the crowd at the Blackhawks' Calder Trophy rally at the United Center on June 13, 2008.

UNITED CENTER

A NEW ERA

Wirtz recalled Comcast officials thought the conversation was about doing one home game.

"I said, no, no, the time is now," Wirtz said. "Tell me how many games can we do? Comcast wasn't used to that kind of speed from us."

Wirtz was right about that.

"I was surprised how fast the transition has occurred," Corno said. "Rocky's been very aggressive. I've admired his aggressiveness."

It was a no-brainer for Wirtz. He felt airing the home games were tantamount to a three-hour commercial.

"I always said the best place to watch the game is inside the United Center," Wirtz said. "But you're not going to get somebody new to go to the United Center and spend X-amount of dollars without at least exposing some of it to them on television. After you watch some of it, you think,

'Hey, that's exciting. Looks good. What it's like in person?' Then once they see it person, they're hooked."

The first of 11 Hawks home games on TV was a Sunday night affair against Detroit in November 2007. The game attracted huge ratings, as fans got their first real glimpses of young stars such as Patrick Kane on Jonathan Toews on home ice.

The buzz was starting to grow for the Hawks.

Wirtz then made his next bold move. He called McDonough and asked for a meeting. They met at a sports bar in Schaumburg just before Thanksgiving. Little did the other patrons know that the future of the Blackhawks was being shaped in their midst. McDonough didn't know it, either.

McDonough, the president of the Cubs, thought Wirtz only wanted to pick his brain. McDonough offered Wirtz advice on the kind of person he should pick for his president.

(Left to right): Blackhawks President John McDonough, Chairman Rocky Wirtz, and Senior Vice President of Business Operations Jay Blunk have guided the transformation of the Blackhawks franchise. (Photo courtesy Sports Business Journal)

INTERVIEW

Meet Season Ticketholder Jim Szymusiak

When did you become a Hawks fan?
Early in the 1960s when I was probably 5–6 years old. To this day I do not know why I got hooked. I had an uncle who was a Chicago police officer and a season tick-etholder. Every home game I would sit by the phone waiting for Uncle Joe to call, and he would call for one game a year. He probably called everyone he knew prior to me!

How long have you been a season ticketholder?
I have been with a group of guys since 1994. I have been officially by myself since about 1995. I started with two, then three children, later I went to four. Probably need to bump that to five.

Who is your all-time favorite Hawk?
It is a toss-up between Bobby Hull and Keith Magnuson. Both of them were impact players on the ice for different reasons. Keith Magnuson was always very friendly to me and my family when he would frequently visit the United Center.

Who is your current favorite Hawk?
Duncan Keith. He was a decent player at Michigan State who through his hard work, dedication, and commitment has made the best of his opportunity playing in the NHL.

Who is your all-time *least* favorite opponent?
Back in the '60s it was Montreal, specifically the clash between Bobby Hull and John Ferguson. Today I would have to go with Detroit.

Greatest Blackhawks memory?
The Hawks winning the Stanley Cup in '61. My grandparents owned a tavern on 53rd and Ashland. The memorabilia provided by Hamm's Beer and other vendors was amazing. I wish I would have saved some of those things.

Why are you most excited about this season?
The real chance for postseason play.

What one offseason change in the past 12 months has had the biggest impact on the Blackhawks' resurgence?
Difficult question. The last 12 months would be the coaching change. The last 24 months would be the addition of the younger players via the draft and the ability of the Hawks and GM Dale Tallon to adjust his team to the new NHL speed/skill.

Do you have a game day/night ritual?
My game day ritual is I wake up with a smile knowing that no matter what life throws at me today I have been blessed with the opportunity to be at a Hawks game that evening. I leave our house at about 3:00 pm to arrive at the United Center prior to 5:30 pm. There always seems to be traffic. The worst traffic days are Sundays when the Bears are home or worse yet is a Bears home game and the Sox in postseason play. I then have a delightful dinner at the Ketel One Club, followed hopefully by a Blackhawks win. To stay awake on the way home I usually listen to the post-game radio show.

"Whoever you have run your business operation, they have to come in with the mindset that they are going to go 0-and-82. Never win a game," McDonough told Wirtz. "Anybody that tells you that you're not drawing because the team is bad isn't the person for you."

Wirtz recalled thinking, "That was music to my ears." He told McDonough that he wanted him to join the Hawks as the new president.

Going into his sales mode, Wirtz said, "This is virgin territory. I think we can make you look really good."

McDonough has always been up for a good challenge. After all, he helped fill Wrigley Field for a team that hadn't won a title for 100 years.

McDonough made it clear that he was taking the same approach to the Hawks. He told the staff the bar had been raised. Shortly after taking the job, McDonough watched the Hawks draw 12,000 fans for a weeknight game in December. He called Tallon and apologized that the Hawks had to play in front of an almost half-empty United Center.

"I sent a message," McDonough said. "I'm not accus-

The 3rd overall pick in the 2006 NHL Entry Draft, Jonathan Toews led all NHL rookies with 24 goals in 2007–08.

tomed to seeing empty seats. We needed to tell Dale there would be no excuses for not filling the building."

Tallon appreciated the commitment from McDonough. "John wanted to get the enthusiasm back for our team," he said.

McDonough worked to put the pieces in place in the front office. He lured his old Cubs associate Jay Blunk to come in as senior vice president of business operations.

"I said to John, 'What do you have over there?'" Blunk said. "He said one word: potential. This place is dripping with potential."

It didn't take long for that potential to start manifesting itself. The young stars were starting to make people notice. McDonough then reached out to the old stars, especially Bobby Hull.

Hull's relationship with the team had soured through the years. All those ill-feelings spilled out when McDonough approached him about coming back to the team as an ambassador. "The conversation was toxic," McDonough said. "It was one of the few times I didn't say anything for 90 minutes. But I had to hear it."

McDonough eventually convinced Hull to meet with Wirtz. The meeting went well, and Hull came away convinced that there was new leadership in place. To celebrate, the Hawks organized special "Welcome Back" nights-for Hull and Stan Mikita, and then one for Tony Esposito. They proved to be emotion-filled evenings for not only the players but also for the fans.

"It helped bring back a generation or two that hadn't been there," McDonough said.

The momentum continued to build. Even though the Hawks barely missed making the playoffs, they attracted crowds in excess of 20,000 for their last three home games.

Then during the offseason, the Hawks not only announced that they were putting all of their home games on TV, they cut a

President John McDonough, Patrick Kane, Chairman Rocky Wirtz, and General Manager Dale Tallon pose with the Calder Trophy, awarded to Kane as the NHL's 2007–08 most outstanding rookie.

deal with their old outlet, WGN Channel 9, to air 20 home and away games. Meanwhile, WGN-720 became the new radio home for the Hawks. McDonough reasoned that for the Hawks to go mainstream, they needed to be in the mainstream. It doesn't get any bigger in Chicago than WGN.

Pat Foley was brought back to call those games on television. It was an extremely popular move for fans who still can hear his trademark "Bannnnneerrrrrmmannn" chant for former Hawks goalie Murray Bannerman.

The Winter Classic was announced with much fanfare. That the NHL would consider the Hawks for such a prestigious national showcase was another validation of how far they had come.

Scotty Bowman also gave a strong endorsement when he joined the Hawks as a senior advisor for hockey operations. The legendary coach said he wouldn't have come on board if he didn't think the Hawks were going in the right direction.

Wirtz was taken aback by what he saw at the Hawks' first fan convention in July. On Saturday, the doors were set to open at 10:00 am. When he arrived at 9:30 am, he encountered fans that had been there since 6:00 am.

"That's when I knew something was going on," Wirtz said. "It was very impressive. The rabid fans wanted to reconnect. All they needed was an excuse to do that. If you allow them to dream and hope, they'll be with you."

The ultimate barometer came in ticket sales. The Hawks jumped from 3,400 season ticketholders to nearly 14,000. The Hawks are expected to play to full houses this year. McDonough was true to his word to Tallon.

New coach Joel Quenneville will be the beneficiary of those fans. A veteran leader with playoff success at St. Louis and Colorado, Quenneville comes in with high expectations.

Reaching back to his old job, McDonough called Quenneville, "a younger version of Lou Piniella." "He's every-day-intense," McDonough said. "He's a man of purpose. He's a winner."

The addition of Quenneville was yet another piece in what truly has been an amazing transformation of the franchise. It is astounding for people who have been around the team for a long time, such as Foley. He gives all the credit to Wirtz.

"Rocky Wirtz didn't just hit a homer," Foley said. "He hit a grand slam."

Blunk says Wirtz now is the most popular owner in sports. He has felt their affection. People stop Wirtz for his autograph. After last season's finale, it took him an hour to make his way through the fans who wanted to thank him for all the changes.

"I couldn't believe it," Wirtz said. "It's been extremely gratifying."

The anticipation is that it will keep getting better for the Hawks. That word, potential, still remains the team's most valuable commodity. It drives everyone in the organization to make sure that potential gets fulfilled.

"I think there's the feeling that we're on the verge of something big," Blunk said. "I know Rocky feels that way. I know the players feel that way."

Blunk then said, "Is this how the Bulls felt before the whole Michael Jordan thing kicked in?"

Perhaps. However, keep in mind, as great as Jordan was, the whole process with the Bulls took time. They had growing pains, too.

Again, that Detroit game on October 25 provided one more important element to add to that microcosm. The Hawks wound up squandering the two-goal lead in the third period, eventually losing 6–5 in a shootout.

The game showed the Hawks and the organization that while they have traveled a long way in a short time, there is still a long way to go.

"We're in the earn-it phase of all this," McDonough said. "We don't take any of this for granted. There is a lot of work to be done. Ultimately, we have to win our way back. And we will." ●

Return to Glory

What was old is new again with the resurgent Blackhawks • By Tim Sassone

Certain courses of action were no-brainers for John McDonough when he took over as president of the Blackhawks.

Putting home games on television? Are you kidding? Check.

Market young stars such as Jonathan Toews, Patrick Kane, Patrick Sharp, Brent Seabrook, and Duncan Keith and put them out in front of the fans as often as possible? Check.

Reconnect with those legends who helped define Blackhawks history?

"That was the first thing, actually," McDonough said.

The calls went out to Bobby Hull, Stan Mikita, and Tony Esposito, Hall of Famers all and possibly the three most popular players in franchise history, even before McDonough had a chance to hang a picture on his office wall.

What McDonough wanted was for the three legends to put aside their old wounds to be ambassadors for the Blackhawks at charity functions and at games, at the rink and away from it, during the season and in the summer.

"We often said it would be very difficult to move forward without really trying to justify what happened in the past," McDonough said. "And the foundation of all these things are Bobby, Stan, Tony, Keith Magnuson, Pierre Pilote, Denis Savard, Glenn Hall – these are part of the pillars of the franchise and you have to be in good standing with them, or try to."

In the cases of Hull, Mikita, and Esposito, at least, somewhere along the way they became disconnected from the franchise for one reason or another and felt they were unwanted.

There was a time when Mike Keenan coached the Hawks and wanted Mikita to go on the ice at practice and help teach the players about faceoffs, having been one of the greatest on draws in NHL history. But the powers that be at that time told Keenan it was out of the question.

Hull simply felt like an outcast, as if his mere presence at either Chicago Stadium or the United Center was a problem for the old ownership. Getting Hull to agree to come back into the family was one of McDonough's toughest tasks.

"The 90 minutes to two hours we spent with Bobby was toxic, profane, painful, difficult to hear, but necessary, and I think it was very therapeutic for him to say that," McDonough said. "When I called him back eight days later to see if we had a chance to reconcile, he said he wanted to come back."

There were no hidden agendas in McDonough reaching out to legends such as Hull, Mikita, and Esposito. He simply knew it was the right thing to do and would help repair the franchise's fractured relationship with its fans.

"I just said to Bobby, you've been estranged from the franchise for almost 36 years and there's going to be a different approach," McDonough said. "Time will tell if it's the right approach, but there's going to be a different approach where we need to embrace our former players.

"Coming from the Cubs, I put a high premium on a relationship with former players so I felt it was very, very important. After Bobby had agreed to come back, Stan and Tony came back quickly thereafter and I explained to them in detail what I would expect their responsibilities to be and they were surprised and flattered that the organization extended themselves officially.

"Each one said they would hear from (the team) from

Blackhawks legends Stan Mikita (left) and Bobby Hull were welcomed back to the Blackhawks family before a game against the San Jose Sharks on March 7, 2008.

time to time, but it was never officially a welcome back and now they've all said individually they all feel they're part of the family again," said McDonough. "We want to maximize their exposure because we think it's good for us."

As soon as Hull, Mikita, and Esposito were named ambassadors last season, they became key components in what has been a storybook turnaround for the franchise.

"I am overwhelmed to be a part of the Chicago Blackhawks family again," Hull said. "I've been away from Chicago for some 35 years, but Chicago was never out of my heart.

"The Chicago Blackhawks logo has always meant a lot to me as I know it does to the Chicago fans. I want to be a part of welcoming and encouraging fans to come out and watch this exciting young team. It was truly time for me to come back to Chicago and I am happy to be back."

Mikita and Esposito have expressed similar sentiments over the past year.

"In my heart, I have always been and always will be a Blackhawk," Esposito said. "I love the new approach the

team is taking. Everything about the Blackhawks is very upbeat and I am proud to be a part of this new beginning."

Whereas Hull, Mikita, and Esposito might not have been welcome around the United Center before, McDonough wants them front and center as often as possible to help celebrate where the franchise has been and where it's going.

"I know why we're here, to bring some of the past back to the Chicago Blackhawks and to the kids," Hull said. "They are a young, young team and I think it's beneficial to them to know what went on prior to today, knowing that for a number of years we were the toughest ticket in town and had such wonderful fans year after year after year."

You can see it in the eyes of the present Hawks, growing wide whenever Hull, Mikita, and Esposito are in the building.

"Obviously, we know they're legendary players," defenseman Duncan Keith said. "It's nice to see them around a little more. It's great for the team, the fans and the organization."

Added captain Jonathan Toews: "We're definitely honored to have a chance to talk to guys like Stan and Bobby

Hall of Fame goaltender and Blackhawks Ambassador Tony Esposito was honored during a pregame ceremony on March 19, 2008.

INTERVIEW

Meet Season Ticketholder David A. Rammelt

When did you become a Hawks fan?
As long as I can remember. My dad started taking me to games when I was 6 or 7 and playing mite hockey. I remember seeing the Chicago cops try to separate Keith Magnuson and an opponent who were in the penalty box fighting (there were no glass partitions in those days); I remember being crushed if Espo wasn't starting in goal; I remember dying to meet Darcy Rota.

How long have you been a season ticketholder?
Since 1992.

Who is your all-time favorite Hawk?
Brutal question. All-around grit and scoring, it has to be Troy Murray. Pure toughness, Probie. Grace, would be Savy.

Who is your current favorite Hawk?
Every one of them is unbelievably nice and approachable. Gotta go with grit and heart—tie between Cam Barker and, as far as I know, the only two-time captain in the storied history of the Wisconsin Badgers, Adam Burish.

Who is your all-time *least* favorite opponent?
St. Louis, since the Wings stopped dropping their gloves. Otherwise, Detroit.

Greatest Blackhawks memory?
I have been really fortunate to have people from the Blackhawks organization do unbelievably nice things for me and my family, from Mr. Wirtz to Bob Pulford to Dale Tallon. If you can imagine this, in all sincerity I have been able to do the following:

1. Check Bob Probert into the boards during a team scrimmage in 1997 (and scored a goal on Jocelyn Thibault, assisted by Casey Hankinson). Thankfully, Probie laughed and did not kill me, and I think I scored while falling on my butt for the 20th time. Never even saw the puck.

2. Listen to Mr. Wirtz tell stories about having the KGB plant bugs in their hotel room at the '72 Summit Series.

3. See my son during the morning skate of a Dallas team road trip shoot breakaways on Corey Crawford this February.

4. Watch my three kids have their photo taken with the team in 2005.

5. Have Dale Tallon swear to give up golf trying to correct my slice during a round of golf.

6. See the Hawks sweep the Wings in the 1991–92 playoffs en route to the Stanley Cup final.

7. Watch the Super Bowl with Bob Pulford, Brian Sutter, and my son in a hotel lounge during a road trip to Montreal in 2004.

8. Listen to the joy of a 13-year-old talk about playing video games with Patrick Kane, Jonathan Toews, and the rest of the guys on the team charter flight to Dallas in 2008.

every day. We'll never forget how special those guys are and what they did for hockey in this city.

"You always have to respect that and keep your own feet on the ground and say no matter what you do, you'll never be the same as those guys."

Second-year winger Patrick Kane saw firsthand at the inaugural Blackhawks fan convention last summer how popular Hull and Mikita still are and got a lesson from them in respecting the fans and being as accessible as possible.

"With Bobby and Stan, just talking to those guys, one of the things about them is they bring so much personality to the game, just the way they act with the fans," Kane said. "They have so much history here and to be involved with them and have them around is really cool."

Stan the Man

Nobody played more games or put more points on the scoreboard than Stan Mikita, the stylish center with the sweet moves and eye-popping passes.

Mikita appeared in 1,394 games over 22 seasons with the Hawks and racked up 1,467 points, 926 of them assists. Mikita was a two-time Hart Trophy winner as league MVP and on four occasions led the NHL in scoring.

Mikita found his break from the Hawks painful considering he has never left the Chicago area since ending his playing days.

"We left when they didn't want us," Mikita said. "I don't think either one of us (with Hull) would ever force ourselves in the dressing room.

"It's been a long wait to be asked back and I am thrilled to accept coming back to the Chicago Blackhawks family. I have been out of hockey for almost 30 years and I still run into fans who remember me. I was 18 years old when I turned pro and I see the same drive and determination when I look at this young Chicago Blackhawks team. I know these young Blackhawks are as excited as I am to be a part of this great organization. I know they want to thrill and excite the fans and bring the Stanley Cup back to Chicago."

Mikita's impact on the sport sometimes gets overlooked. He was the first Czechoslovakian-born player to appear in the NHL and was the all-time leader in points among European-

THE COACH

Quenneville's Quest to Win

Rarely is a coach with the experience, knowledge, and skill level that Joel Quenneville possesses available to be hired. When he was, the Blackhawks moved quickly to ensure the man with 438 career victories under his belt was in the fold to help guide an up-and-coming young team to the next level.

Quenneville was named the 37th head coach in Hawks history on October 16, 2008, after a short stint as a professional scout with the team. In Quenneville, the Hawks hired a former NHL coach of the year with a .592 career winning percentage who has guided his teams to the postseason nine times in 11 seasons.

"The Blackhawks have always been a team I idolized growing up as a young boy," the 50-year-old Quenneville says. "It's something to be proud of to be a part of this tradition. Hopefully we can recapture the days where they had a lot of success here.

"I'm fortunate to be here. Hockey enthusiasm has returned here, we have a young team that has ability, and it's a great opportunity to be a part of it. We're at a stage here as a team and organization that we feel we're on the right path and we want to keep going forward."

Quenneville served as head coach of the St. Louis Blues from 1996–2004 and Colorado Avalanche from 2005–08. He led the Blues to a career-best 51 victories during the 1999–2000 season when the team captured the President's Trophy with the league's best record. That was the season he was awarded the Jack Adams Trophy as the league's top coach.

That impressive résumé is what drew the Hawks to him.

"Joel brings us a wealth of experience and a winning track record that will have an immediate and lasting impact," general manager Dale Tallon says.

Quenneville is one of three men in the history of the NHL to have played in and coached 800 games. The former top pick (21st overall) of the Toronto Maple Leafs in the 1978 amateur draft appeared in 13 seasons as a defenseman beginning in 1979 with the Leafs, Colorado Rockies, New Jersey Devils, Hartford Whalers, and Washington Capitals.

With the Hawks appeared poised to join the upper-echelon of the NHL, Quenneville's coaching philosophy could help them reach new heights.

"I like to say we're an up-tempo type of team," Quenneville says. "We like to be hard- working, we like to be simple, clear and organized." ●

—*Chris Kuc*

born players until he was passed by Jaromir Jagr.

Mikita also was credited with inventing the curved hockey stick.

McDonough never will forget the night of March 7, 2008, when Mikita and Hull were formally welcomed back into the Blackhawks family during a goosebump-raising ceremony at the United Center.

"The night that we honored the two of them here, I really believe that was a watershed defining moment in the franchise history," McDonough said. "It was almost as if our fan base was embracing them, and most people didn't believe this would ever be reconciled, ever."

The Golden Jet

Before Michael Jordan owned Chicago, Bobby Hull did.

When Hull played for the Hawks from 1957 through 1972 he held rock-star status. Hull was mobbed everywhere he went, home and road, and never did he turn down a request for an autograph. The fans loved Bobby and he loved them right back.

Why, there were times during the pregame skate when Hull could be spotted signing autographs for kids hanging over the glass.

Hull was a powerful figure on the ice. He could go end-to-end with the puck or pull up and take one of the hardest slap shots in the history of the game. Hull was a two-time MVP, three-time scoring champ, and is the Hawks' all-time goal-scoring leader with 604.

"It's indelible in my mind when I'd go around the net and grab the biscuit, I could feel the people getting out of their seats," Hull said. "The further I got, the faster I went and the more they got out of their seats. By the time I was at the blue line ready to crank one up they were up and skating every stride with me.

"A lot of guys say they are oblivious to the crowd, but I remember every time I went on the ice, I knew those 22,000 people were skating every stride with me," Hull said. "I was fortunate enough to come to the greatest city in the world with the greatest fans in the world. I spent 15 years here and I thought that's all I was going to get out of it, but time went by and here I am getting a second chance."

It seemed as if all was right in the world again once Hull became part of the organization again.

"Bobby was very suspect of why I was calling," McDonough said. "Rocky (Wirtz) and I ultimately met with him because he needed to hear it coming from Rocky, too. It was really important that it was from a Wirtz."

Last summer Hull was honored by the NHL as the Alumni of the Year, making his return to the Hawks complete.

"He seems genuinely happy to be back," McDonough said. "He's in a very good place. He feels, and he'll tell you this, that he is respected again, and I think that's an important word to those gentlemen."

Tony O

Can any Hawks fans ever forget those cold nights at Chicago Stadium when the chants of "To-ny, To-ny" would rain down from the rafters?

Tony Esposito seemingly came out of nowhere to become a rookie star with the Hawks in 1969–70 after being claimed for $25,000 from the Montreal Canadiens.

Esposito won the Calder Trophy as rookie of the year in '69–70 after he went 38–17–8 with a 2.17 goals-against average. Not only that, he set an NHL record that still stands today with an astounding 15 shutouts.

Esposito is the franchise leader with 74 shutouts and 418 career victories.

"It's a great honor to be asked back into the Blackhawks family," Esposito said. "In my heart, I have always been and always will be a Blackhawk. I love the new approach the team is taking. Everything about the Blackhawks is very upbeat and I am proud to be a part of this new beginning."

It's a new beginning now with strong and firm roots to the past with Esposito, Mikita, and Hull back in the team picture.

"As we're trying to rebuild this thing and re-energize this fan base and rejuvenate this, this was an important part," McDonough said. "If we had been rebuffed by Bobby, Stan, Tony, and others, I would have been able to understand it. But it is about respect and communication and we will continue to have a good relationship with all of these people we have honored going forward." ●

Joel Quenneville took over as head coach on October 16, 2008. Quenneville, formerly the bench boss for St. Louis and Colorado, made the playoffs in nine of his 10 full seasons as head coach for the Blues and Avalanche.

YOUNG GUNS

Kane and Toews Energize Blackhawks

By Chris Kuc

In the long and storied history of the Chicago Blackhawks, some players have transcended all others to have their names become synonymous with the Indian head.

Bobby Hull, Stan Mikita, Tony Esposito, Pierre Pilote, and Glenn Hall, among others, will forever be linked with the Hawks. And now two young players appear poised to add their names to the pantheon of hockey on the West side of Chicago: Patrick Kane and Jonathan Toews.

The youngsters are adding a new chapter to the Hawks' history book as the cornerstones for the rebirth of a franchise now in its 82nd season.

Like the legendary players before them, Kane and Toews are more than just skilled players on the ice. They are more than slap shots, cross-ice passes, and back checks. They are players who have embraced playing for an Original Six franchise and have become the new faces of the Blackhawks.

After the malaise of a decade filled mostly with missed postseason opportunities and a sag in attendance that followed, the Hawks' fortunes got a jump-start at the 2006 NHL Entry Draft when general manager Dale Tallon pounced on the opportunity to select Jonathan Toews, who was successfully leading the University of North Dakota and Team Canada's Under-20 squad, with the third overall selection.

A little bit of luck raised the team's fortunes when it won the '07 draft lottery and was awarded the first pick. An undersized kid from Buffalo who was setting rookie scoring records

with London of the Ontario Hockey League grabbed the team's attention and the Patrick Kane era began in Chicago.

"It's just one of the greatest organizations," Kane said. "When you look at it, they haven't won a Stanley Cup in a while and you want to come in and help them win. They haven't been around the top teams in the league and hockey kind of went away from this city. To come into this situation where you can help rebuild and help make hockey in Chicago a successful thing to be part of is really enjoyable.

"It seems like we're the faces of the franchise. To be in a situation to help them turn the corner is a privilege. I couldn't really be in a better situation with an Original Six team as the team was rebuilding and it needed young players to come in and maybe turn around the team and the city. It was a perfect situation for me and also for Jonathan, too."

Toews agreed, "It's one of those things we were kind of were born into when we were drafted and came to our first training camp. High expectations were already there and everyone maybe thought we were players who could make a difference. We were on that first team that kind of represented hope for hockey in the city. People wanted to get excited about that and wanted to get excited about what this team could do.

"For Patrick and me, it was definitely special to be considered players who make a big difference. We're excited and honored about the position we're in."

It didn't take long to see the pair would be something

Jonathan Toews was named team captain in July 2008 at the inaugural Blackhawks Convention. At 20 years and 79 days old, Toews became the third-youngest captain in league history, behind Sidney Crosby and Vincent Lecavalier.

special as they took the ice together at Prospects Camp '07 and quickly showed exceptional talent. The rest, as they say, is history. Or the making of it.

It was October 19, 2007, that Hawks fans and the rest of the National Hockey League got a glimpse of something special happening in the Windy City.

Early in the game against the Colorado Avalanche that night, the then-19-year-old Toews brought the United Center crowd to its feet when he weaved his way through three defenders and beat goaltender Jose Theodore for the goal of the year not only for the Hawks but the entire league.

"It's kind of weird when I think of it," Toews said. "It was only a couple of games into my first season and I'd only scored a handful of goals like that in my career but not at

this level. It was a special play I like to remember."

Also worth remembering is later in that game, won by the Hawks 5–3, when an 18-year-old Kane scored his first career NHL goal in front of boyhood hero Joe Sakic.

"I had three points that game and we ended up winning and I was named No. 1 star and Sakic was named second star," Kane said. "It was really cool when you're playing against a guy you kind of idolize growing up and you score your first goal that game and then you're first star and he's second."

Since early in that 2007–08 season, Kane and Toews have been inseparable on the ice and close friends off it. Having a fellow teenager to go through the rigors of a rookie season helped the development of both players.

"Since the beginning it's been Kane and Toews or Toews and Kane," said Kane, who won the Calder Trophy as the

Patrick Kane and fellow Calder Trophy finalist Jonathan Toews sign autographs for fans as they arrive for the 2008 NHL Awards in Toronto, Canada. (Photo by Bruce Bennett/Getty Images for NHL)

league's rookie of the year in 2007–08. "We've just done everything together, from rooming on the road to sitting next to each other in the locker room. Everything seems to be together with us. It's been really fortunate because you can always lean on someone on and off the ice. It gives you some knowledge of what is going on in another person's life and who's basically in the same situation as you."

"We have that special bond that we shared our rookie seasons together," Toews said. "We went through a lot of the same things together. Every day we're on the same line and doing the same things. Sometimes it's not easy, so it's always good to have the other guy pick you up some days when you don't feel like going to work."

Kane and Toews took different paths to the NHL, but they share a common thread in their development into NHL's stars—family. Both players had unwavering support from parents who nurtured their sons' abilities and desires to play hockey at young ages.

Kane, born November 19, 1988, in Buffalo, credits his parents, Patrick Sr. and Donna, with sacrificing much of their time to his hockey career.

"Family starts it off," Kane said. "Your parents have to really help you with a lot off the ice. They've been great for me.

"I started a little bit later than most kids. I was seven years old when I came in and my dad said I just kept getting better every time I skated on the ice. It's funny watching clips of my first game. I'm awful and then a year later I'm coming in and kind of going though the whole other team and making nice plays."

At 14, Kane made the decision that helped shape his life and hockey career. He moved to Detroit to play for Honeybaked, a AAA junior team, and lived with former NHL player Pat Verbeek.

"That's when I really took a chance and realized I wanted to play hockey for my life and have it as a career," said the 5'10", 175-pound Kane. "I then was fortunate enough to play in the U.S. program and that worked out well.

I went to London for a year and that worked out really well as it took me from a third-rounder to first-overall pick and here I am in the NHL. It couldn't have worked out better."

Two seasons with the United States National Top Development Team and a remarkable rookie season in London where he had 62 goals and 83 assists in 58 games brought Kane to the attention of the Blackhawks.

Toews, born April 29, 1988, in Winnipeg, Manitoba, put on skates not long after he began walking. His father, Bryan, built a rink in the backyard of their home for Jonathan and his brother David—a third-round draft pick (66th overall) of the New York Islanders in 2008—to learn the game.

"My dad had the biggest influence on me," Jonathan Toews said. "He put a stick in my hands when I was very young and he got my first pair of skates when I was three or four. By the time I was five years old I started playing on a team and making friends. My dad started building a rink when I was five or six, and every winter from then on until I was about 14 years old we had a rink in the backyard and that's where I spent my time and where my dream of playing in the NHL was born."

Toews' mother, Andrée Gilbert, was also instrumental in the center's development not only skill-wise but in temperament as well.

"It was my parents who influenced me to work hard and be the best I can be in hockey," Toews said. "At a very young age I knew I wanted to play in the NHL. It probably wasn't until I was 13 or 14 when I started to feel that at every level I wanted to be the best player. Eventually I felt playing in the NHL could be a reality."

At 15, his parents enrolled him at Shattuck-St. Mary's Prep in Faribault, Minnesota, and Toews blossomed with 48 goals and 62 assists for 110 points in 64 games. From there he attended the University of North Dakota, where as a sophomore he was the team's assistant captain. Then came the 2007 draft and the donning of a Hawks sweater for the first time.

"It's just always been my drive at every level to be one of the best players," said Toews, who was named the captain

Martin Havlat looks on as Patrick Kane celebrates a goal at home against Detroit on October 25, 2008.

of the Hawks at age 20, the third-youngest in NHL history. "Every time I'd be on a bigger stage, whether it was my own neighborhood, the city of Winnipeg, and then eventually in western Canada, I always felt like I was at the top and one of the best players, and if I wasn't I was motivated to get there. I think that's what kept me around and gave me the chance to play in the NHL."

"The great thing about those two kids is sometimes you have to be careful with kids drafted first, second, or third—there might be egos involved or maybe even a little envy," Tallon said. "That's been far from the case. The great thing is that not only are they good players and different players and they complement each other on and off the ice, they really genuinely like each other. That makes it easy."

A close friendship has developed between the two despite nearly opposite demeanors. Toews is aptly nick-named "Mr. Serious" by his teammates while Kane or "Kaner" is happy-go-lucky.

"With how serious he is and maybe how serious I'm not, it's why we gel," Kane said. "It's almost like saying opposites attract. We're really good friends off the ice and we seem to gel on the ice. He's great. He really loves hockey, he loves the game. You can really look up to that with how hard he works. I'd love to play on the same team with him for a while."

"He's incredibly skilled and he's creative," Toews said of Kane. "A lot of times you look at him off the ice or even standing there in his equipment it's tough to believe he can do the things he does. He's really smart and makes things

Jonathan Toews' teammates congratulate him on a goal. Despite missing 18 games with a knee injury last season, Toews finished second on the team with 24 goals, behind only Patrick Sharp's 36.

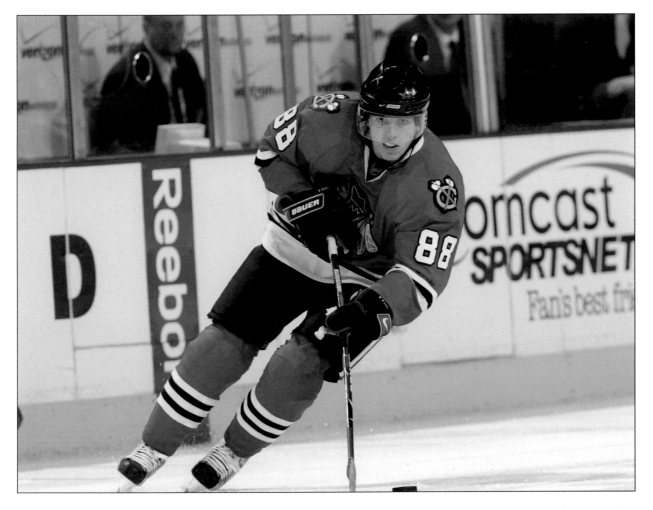

happen. A lot of times I'd be dumping the puck in or making safe plays but he's always looking for something there."

The presence of Kane and Toews has helped lift the organization's profile around the league and free agents are now calling the Hawks about joining the franchise.

"Those guys are probably the head of the class when you talk about good young players," said defenseman Brian Campbell, who signed an eight-year, free-agent contract with the Hawks to help form a talented core with Kane and Toews. "I want to win. I believe they're quality players who can do that. That's a big reason why I'm here.

"When you grow up you look at those Original Six teams, there's a lot of history there. We can do really good things here over a period of time."

For now, though, it's Kane and Toews who are growing up on and off the ice in front of the watchful eyes of some of the most passionate fans in hockey.

"They are two high-caliber cornerstones to our organization," Dale Tallon said. "I've always said they're probably the Hull and Mikita of our era. That's what built the franchise originally and I think [Kane and Toews] are just going to get better and better, bigger and stronger. In a couple of years from now they're going to be dominant players." ●

Patrick Kane set the Blackhawks' rookie record with 51 assists in 2007–08. Combined with his 21 goals, Kane led all rookies in points (72).

Brian Campbell

#	Player	Height	Weight	DOB	Age	Birthplace
51	Brian Campbell	6' 0"	188	May 23, 1979	29	Strathroy, ON, CAN

As one of the biggest free-agent prizes of the offseason, defenseman Brian Campbell signed the richest deal in Blackhawks history—eight years, $56 million—to become the leader of the team's power-play unit. But because he's the third-oldest skater on the team at the ripe old age of 29, he's also picked up the title of "team leader and mentor" in his short tenure with the Hawks.

"I hope the guys feel they can ask me questions and I can try to make sure things are alright with them away from the rink," Campbell says. "There are lots of things that you can do away from the rink that can make a team stronger."

Campbell can play the advisor role to a lot of the Blackhawks players because he's done it all before. As a sixth-round pick by Buffalo in 1997, he's had to work his way up to even be considered a solid prospect. He worked to earn his ice time at every level. He's found success and has lived with the pressure of being an All-Star every game. Most importantly, he played for two NHL teams that went deep into the playoffs—Buffalo in 2006 and 2007 and San Jose in 2008—and he knows how to keep a locker room at ease even in the most pressured situations.

"We have fun," says Campbell of his new team. "I've been through a little bit before but I don't really think that I act 'old.' I think it's good just to stay loose and have some fun."

But Campbell's also aware that his legacy as a Blackhawk and how the team is perceived will eventually be judged on wins and losses.

"I don't think the expectations were very high in previous years, so it's about learning how to handle those expectations," says Campbell. "Right now, we're learning how to win games. It's not just going to be 'ho-hum, we didn't make the playoffs this year.' There are expectations and the goals that we have set out for us this year are reasonable and attainable. It's not alright to fail." ●

Above: GM Dale Tallon (left) introduces Brian Campbell to the Chicago media after signing an eight-year contract with the Blackhawks. Right: Campbell is known as one of the NHL's best offensive defensemen, and was tied for third among defensemen in points in 2007–08 (62).

With his blazing speed and puckhandling skills, Campbell
was brought in to quarterback the Blackhawks' power play.

Cristobal Huet

#	PLAYER	HEIGHT	WEIGHT	DOB	AGE	BIRTHPLACE
38	CRISTOBAL HUET	6' 1"	205	SEPT 3, 1975	33	ST-MARTIN-D'HÈRES, FRA

Goaltender Cristobal Huet certainly had plenty of offers from other teams when he hit the free-agent market last summer; when you win 11 of your last 13 starts for a team that wins their division, all in your walk year, you're bound to spark interest. But when the Blackhawks called on him, he knew he had had to listen closely to their offer.

"The commitment the Hawks made and the fact that they're an Original Six team [drew me to Chicago]," explains Huet. "All of those factors combined to help me pick this city."

With Huet between the pipes, Washington clinched the NHL's Southeast Division after ending the first half of the season in 14th place in the Eastern Conference. Huet was lights-out for Washington, going 11–2–0 with two shutouts and a goal-against average of just 1.63.

In his five previous NHL seasons, Huet posted a sterling 83–61–14 record and never gave up more than 2.81 goals per game. For Huet, winning isn't just a passion—it's a habit.

Huet says that he sees the same kind of winning potential for Chicago, and adds that a postseason run could be in the team's near future.

"We might have a run someday," he says. "I think it takes a lot to get there. Everything's very competitive now. It takes grit and will to be in the big dance."

Huet considers his positioning and consistency his biggest assets in the net, but sums up his purpose very simply: "[When] I stop the puck," says Huet, "that's the best thing I can do for the team."

By signing him to a four-year contract, the Hawks have committed their future to Huet, and have insured that he will be stopping pucks for the team for a long time. After all, every team's foundation should be a goalie who has made winning a habit. ●

Above: Cristobal Huet poses with GM Dale Tallon at a United Center press conference on August 4, 2008. Right: Huet helped the Washington Capitals make the playoffs last season by winning 11 of 13 starts after being traded from Montreal.

"Everything's very competitive now," says Huet. "There are some really good teams in our division. It takes grit to get into the playoffs and compete there."

Winter at Wrigley

There will be no ivy, but plenty of ice • by Len Ziehm

It started out as a lark, just a well-meaning Canadian attempt to create a unique hockey moment. But the first regular season outdoor game in National Hockey League history turned out to be much more than that.

The Edmonton Oilers and Montreal Canadiens squared off at Edmonton's Commonwealth Stadium on November 22, 2003, in a game much more significant than the Canadiens' 4–3 victory that it produced. Temperatures dropped below zero during the game witnessed by 57,167 fans. Right then and there what was then called the NHL Heritage Classic achieved its goal. It created a happy memory, and a tradition was born.

"Every guy (who played) knows how special that moment was," said then-Montreal defenseman Sheldon Souray. "It's something that we can look back on at the end of our careers and be proud that we were a part of it."

"Looking in the stands and seeing that many people was such a big thrill," added Edmonton's Shawn Horcoff in the aftermath of that game. "It was something that will probably never happen again."

Well, Horcoff was wrong.

That outdoor game was so well received the NHL was pressured to hold another one. It took four years for that to happen, but now the concept is likely an annual thing and Chicago and the Blackhawks will be next up to bat.

With John McDonough campaigning almost from his first day as Hawks' president, the club landed this year's Winter Classic. It'll be held at Wrigley Field on January 1, 2009,

against the Detroit Red Wings—a most appropriate opponent. They've formed the longest-standing rivalry in the NHL, with the New Year's Day clash the 701st regular-season matchup between the teams. Number 700 will be played on December 30 at Joe Louis Arena, but that milestone meeting won't draw near the attention the outdoor battle will.

This Winter Classic will be the first held in a baseball stadium. The other two were in football arenas. Chicago's will have the smallest attendance. There were 71,217 on hand at Buffalo's Ralph Wilson Stadium on January 1, 2008, when the Pittsburgh Penguins topped the host Sabres 2–1 in a shootout. Wrigley Field, however, can only seat about 42,000.

The Winter Classic, though, isn't about attendance. If it were this one could have been held at the University of Michigan's Stadium, which seats over 100,000. The Winter Classic is about observing traditions. And if any sports arena abounds in tradition, it's Wrigley Field.

"The cathedral of baseball," said Jim Devellano, senior vice president of both the Wings and baseball's Detroit Tigers. "It'll be a tremendous spectacle, and the Wings are very excited to be part of it."

"It was an absolute highlight last year, and I expect it to be terrific again, being in an iconic venue that has history and tradition," NHL commissioner Gary Bettman said.

"This will be one of the most exciting moments in our history," added Cubs chairman Crane Kenney.

Wrigley Field opened in 1914 and has been the Cubs

The National Hockey League acknowledged the resurgence of the Chicago Blackhawks by awarding them the NHL Winter Classic 2009, which will be played New Year's Day at historic Wrigley Field in Chicago.

home since 1916. It was the home for football's Chicago Bears from 1921–70, and the Chicago Sting, a North American Soccer League powerhouse of the 1980s, also played there. Wrigley additionally hosted boxing, rodeos, and ski-jumping, and recent non-sports offerings including four sellout concerts by Jimmy Buffett (2005) and The Police (2007).

How the Game Came About

Other Chicago venues were considered for this Winter Classic, but Soldier Field had a potential conflict with a possible Bears playoff game and a variety of reasons ruled out using U.S. Cellular Field, home of the White Sox. The bottom line was that McDonough's diligence and the charm of Wrigley Field won out with the NHL hierarchy.

This was to be a year for the Winter Classic to be played in a baseball stadium, with Yankee Stadium the odds-on early favorite. Construction issues there, however, required a different site.

"Chicago's a great sports town, and the revival of the Blackhawks along with this magnificent historical land-

mark was a great combination," said Bettman, who kicked off the Winter Classic festivities at a well-attended media event at Wrigley Field on July 22, two days after the inaugural Blackhawks Convention completed its successful three-day run.

McDonough, stunned to see the configuration of a hockey rink in the Wrigley Field outfield in his first visit back to the park since his resignation as Cubs president, predicted the Winter Classic will be "one of the toughest regular season tickets—if not THE toughest—to secure in the history of Chicago sports."

So why does such a game draw such interest?

"It's the novelty of playing with the elements and history," said Scotty Bowman, the legendary coach who directed the Wings and now works as an advisor for the Hawks. "Hockey's an indoor sport, but kids start playing it outdoors."

The Setup

Putting on a game like this isn't easy. Weather is always a concern, but the NHL is getting good at it. Personnel from all

Wrigley Field has been home to the Chicago Cubs and Chicago Bears, but has never hosted a hockey game until the NHL Winter Classic.

30 teams will be used on the project, with Dan Craig, the NHL facilities operations manager, in charge. Craig made some changes in preparation from last year's game in Buffalo.

Last year the league worked with a contracted company to build the floor for the rink and rented the refrigeration units. This year the league is building its own floor and buying the refrigeration units, a clear indication the game is being targeted as an annual extravaganza.

The floor will consist of five aluminum plates put together like a jigsaw puzzle. They'll be manufactured in Anaheim, California, and are scheduled to arrive at Wrigley Field on December 17.

A change in construction schedule is also in the works. Last year the crew gathered in Buffalo on December 22 but couldn't begin work until the Buffalo Bills concluded their season against the New York Giants. All those people had to work through Christmas non-stop to have things ready.

This time they'll go home for Christmas because the floor can be built before then. Craig said the building of the floor is the biggest challenge involved in the project, especially the first inch of ice. The ideal temperature for making ice is 25 degrees Fahrenheit. Whether Craig and his crew get that remains to be seen.

"When the ice is too cold it becomes brittle," said Craig. "If the temperature gets below the 18-degree mark other challenges arise. Ice freezes from the top down, instead of from the bottom up, so 'shell ice' forms when the temperature is too cold. 'Shell ice' doesn't allow one surface to bind to the other. When a player skates on shell ice, the ice flakes away from the skate blade."

A standard NHL indoor rink has ice that is one to one and a quarter inches thick.

"The most important aspect with this project is making the rink and ice safe for the players," Craig said.

Members of the Blackhawks, both past and present, spent time in the Cubs' clubhouse prior to the start of the NHL Winter Classic 2009 press conference.

Once the foundation is set the crew can enjoy a brief holiday break. When the crew returns on December 26 all it'll have to do is build up the ice, seal it, paint it, flood it, and skate on it.

The players on the Hawks and Wings won't get to see much of it, though. They will likely get just one practice on the outdoor rink. But that's all the Sabres and Penguins had a year ago and their game turned out just fine.

The Uniforms

Because the game is a once-in-a-lifetime event, each team will wear commemorative retro jerseys. The Hawks' will be primarily black with red and beige horizontal body stripes. That was the style worn in 1936–37. Detroit will wear a white-based jersey with a single red body stripe inspired by the jerseys worn by the club in 1926–27. The crest features a classic Old English "D" in the center with the current team's winged logo on each shoulder.

"By wearing commemorative retro jerseys, we not only are celebrating the history of these two Original Six teams, but also recognizing the uniqueness of bringing the game back to its roots," said Brian Jennings, the NHL's executive vice president of marketing.

The Players

Because the outdoor game is such a unique experience, the players are caught up in the novelty of it all. The only exception might be Ty Conklin, one of the Wings' goaltenders. He was a participant in both the games at Edmonton and Buffalo. Brian Campbell, the Hawks' defenseman, not only played for the Sabres but scored in last year's game.

Hawks' winger Adam Burish, though, played in an outdoor game before either of those two. His University of Wisconsin team played in such a game at Lambeau Field in Green Bay, Wisconsin, on February 11, 2006. That one was called the Frozen Tundra Classic and drew 40,890 spectators. Wisconsin came out the winner, 4–2 over Ohio State, as

temperatures hit a balmy 26 degrees.

"It was so different, something I'll always remember," Burish said. "It's the experience. You could put gravel out there for us to play on, and we'll find a way to have fun with it. The surface probably won't be great. Lambeau got chopped up really fast and if it snows it'll be even worse— but who cares? We're here for the great event and put a good show on for the fans."

The History

For the record, there have been other outdoor games. The first involving NHL teams was on September 28, 1991, when the New York Rangers and Los Angeles Kings met in a preseason game outside Caesars Palace in Las Vegas. That game drew 13,000, and many watched in shorts and T-shirts since temperatures reached 80 degrees. Wayne Gretzky played for the Kings in that one.

"We were a little bit in awe, and I'm sure (the Rangers) were, too," said Gretzky. "We kept looking at each other and couldn't believe we were playing in 80-degree weather. But it was nice."

The biggest crowd for an outdoor game didn't involve NHL teams. On October 6, 2001, Michigan and Michigan State kicked off the collegiate season before 74,554 at East Lansing, Michigan. This one was called "The Cold War" and ended in a 3–3 tie.

Red Berenson, the former NHL player and then Michigan head coach, was impressed with how well that game turned out and predicted more such games.

"I thought I'd seen everything in hockey," Berenson said. "But it couldn't have turned out better. It was pretty obvious that it was something people would look at in the future for big games. Unlike the previous outdoor games, Chicago's Winter Classic will bring together two of the NHL's Original Six teams."

The Hawks and Wings played for the 698th time at the United Center on October 26 with the Wings winning 6–5 in

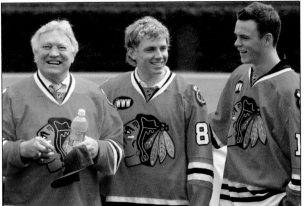

a shootout. They'll square off again at Joe Louis Arena on December 6 and December 30 before heading for Chicago.

In their regular season meetings, the Wings have won 353 games, while the Hawks have recorded 261 victories with 84 ties. There have been 344 regular season games played in Chicago. This doesn't count Chicago home games played against Detroit in Indianapolis and St. Louis in the 1950s or another played in Detroit in 1929 because of bad ice in Chicago. The Hawks have won 159 of their home games, Detroit has won 136 and 49 ended in a tie after regulation play.

These longtime rivals have also met 69 times in playoff games, Detroit winning 38 and the Hawks 31. In playoff games played in Chicago the Hawks have won 24 and the Wings 10. But their Winter Classic meeting won't be like any of the others.

Tuning In

While getting tickets for the Winter Classic will be no small task, watching it won't be difficult. NBC will broadcast the game live in the U.S. In Canada CBC and RDS will provide the TV coverage. NHL Radio on Westwood One will provide coverage for stations across North America, and NHL.com will offer extensive digital video coverage. College football bowl games may dominate the airwaves on this New Year's Day, but the Winter Classic is sure to gather more than its share of viewers and listeners.

"What a way to start the new year, with two of the storied names in hockey playing in one of America's venerable stadiums," said NBC Sports president Ken Schanzer.

"This game will certainly be a career highlight for the players on both teams," summed up Paul Kelly, executive director of the NHL Players Association. ●

With the distinctive Wrigley scoreboard providing a picturesque backdrop, members of the media conducted interviews with Blackhawks personnel following the press conference.

Fan Q&A with Hull & Mikita

HawkCast, the Official Blackhawks Podcast, March 7, 2008

Adam Kemperaar, HawkCast Host: How were you approached by Rocky Wirtz and John McDonough to come back as ambassadors, and what was your reaction when you heard from them?

Stan: Actually, I was surprised about getting a phone call from management first of all, and the other thing was [the offer] to come back and still be considered one of the Blackhawks. To be able to mingle with the new kids if I wanted to, which I have; and mingle with our alumni guys, which I have also done. I was really surprised that somebody would do that after we have not been asked for quite a while.

AK: Bobby, you were at the game Wednesday (March 5, 2008) night against Anaheim. You appeared on the scoreboard and got a great reaction. What has the reaction been since it was announced that you guys were going to be coming back into the fold?

Bobby: Everyone that I have talked to has been so positive about Stan, Tony, and I being back in the fold. As you know we spent the prime of our lives [here], Stan was here for 23 years I believe and I was in Chicago for 15 years before I left the city. It's the greatest city in the world and I thought this was my one go, my one kick at the cat, and here it is 35 or so years later and we're getting another go at it — and you just can't imagine the feeling knowing that you're wanted again after all of those years.

AK: When you think of the Chicago Stadium what is the first thing that comes to your mind?

Stan: I think of the National Anthem, the way it was started at the old stadium where the fans just started chanting a little, no one really sang the anthem with the singer before that. Then all of a sudden one section started and it was like a crescendo starting. I think to top it off was the All-Star Game in the old stadium — I think it was 1991 during Desert Storm.

Bobby: Chicago Stadium was the greatest sphere of action of any rink that I have ever played in, and I believe the reason for that is the configuration of the building. The fans were out over top of us. The mezzanine and boxes went back a short way and then the first balcony came out over top of them, and then second balcony went out over top of the first balcony, and the people were right on top of us. They weren't so far back that they couldn't be a part of the game. Every person in the old Chicago Stadium was a part of our action and as Stan said that the noise was deafening. I know I sat up underneath the first balcony that day of Desert Storm when the All-Star Game was here and I sat right next to Billy Reay. And when they started roaring during the anthem and after it finished I turned to Billy and whispered in his ear because you couldn't hear yourself think. I said, "Was it this loud when we played?" And he said, "Bobby, when you and Stan would get three [goals] the roof would come off this building."

Hawks legend Stan Mikita holds a number of Blackhawks team records, including games played (1,394) and career points (1,467), and is the only player in NHL history to win the Art Ross and Lady Byng Trophies in the same season (1966–67 and 1967–68).

AK: Let's get to some fan questions now...Brad in Chicago wants to know what are your fondest memories of playing together in Chicago?

Stan: We didn't really play together as a unit very often. Usually we got together on the power play and killing penalties, so that is the only time we saw each other. On the regular shift we had our own lines that we played with. I had an outfit called the Scooter Line—I don't know who gives out these names, but I had Kenny Wharram out there on the right wing who could really scoot, and of course Bobby played on that famous Million Dollar Line, and I don't know what that stood for. Bobby, could you enlighten me a little bit on it?

Bobby: I don't know, I know we never got a million dollars.

Stan: Well wait a minute, I know he did but not during that time.

Randy Johnson, Sacramento, CA: This is a little fantasy question here, the two of you discover the fountain of youth and are making a comeback for the Hawks, which current player on the team is the third man on your line?

Bobby: With Stanley at center, anyone could be wingers playing with him. I would expect one of those Kane or Toews kids because they are great athletes, great skaters, can handle the puck really well, they know the ice, they know the game, and they would be fun to play with. Stan, would you take center and make Jonathan play the wing?

Stan: I would play anywhere and the way he goes around he could play anywhere. I don't think because you're named to a position you really do that because you cover for each other and when the play changes direction you have to fill in wherever you have to. You play as a hockey player not as a position player.

Michael Lewandowski, Oswego, IL: Which player did you not look forward to seeing across the faceoff circle the most and why?

Stan: Oh I don't know, I always enjoyed the people I played against. It was always a challenge, and I knew they were as tough as nails because that's what you tried to be, speaking for myself, and it didn't matter really. I had some good contests against guys like Hank Richard, you probably remember him as Henri Richard, and Bobby Clark was another. They were all different players but you always had competition against those guys and I really enjoyed it.

AK: Bobby, I am sure like Stan you were not intimidated by anyone, but was there anyone like the guys Stan mentioned where you thought, 'Wow this is going to be a tough night?'

Bobby: I believe some of the greatest games that I was ever involved in was in the old Olympia in Detroit, playing head-on-head with a guy named Gordon Howe. He was somewhat intimidating but we had kind of a mutual admiration society where he knew that I wanted to play the game within the rules and I was going to let him do the same. So it was up-and-down, up-and-down all night. They didn't like me in Detroit that well, they called me the sweat hog. I think that was because Stan, the night before we used to fill the tanks with a little bit of Stroh's, that fire-brewed beer, and our red crimson jersey used to get snappin' in the breeze—some of the greatest games I ever played in against the old Detroit Red Wings in the Olympia.

Jeff Reid, North Bay, Ontario: Today's players are happy to shoot the puck at 100 miles per hour, the record I think is 105 mph, Bobby's shot was clocked at 118.3 mph. How come it was so much faster? So for both Bobby and Stan who do you think is the hardest shot of all time and why?

Stan: Bobby Hull. I have never seen any faster, any harder because there hasn't been.

Bobby: They tried to compare Dennis' and my shot, my brother Dennis. They said that likely I could shoot the puck through a car wash without it getting wet. Dennis could shoot the puck every bit as hard if not harder but he just couldn't hit the car wash.

Caitlyn Tyrrell, St. Charles, IL: How do you think the game has changed since you have played and for better or for worse?

Stan: Other than the money factor, that is probably the main issue and God bless them, the kids who are making that money. The only thing that I see is that the people are getting bigger but society gets bigger and so every sport has bigger [players]. I don't know if they are any tougher. I think the fights are still of equal results, the bigger guy usually wins, the stronger guy, but I really don't see much of a difference—you still have to put the puck in the net, and the guy that can do it the slickest I think is the winner.

Bobby: I believe the kids today Stan, are bigger, stronger and maybe skate a little faster and shoot a little harder, but I question them playing all over the ice. There are a lot of one-dimensional players and Stan moved the puck around from one end to the other via passing the puck and getting it back and giving it and taking it away and making

the defense back up until his wingers could scoot in from either side. Now to get somebody that can handle the puck and make a play sometimes is lacking out there. There are a lot of one-dimensional players. We had to play all over the ice because there were just six teams. Only 120 supposedly of the best players and they all had to be well-rounded and play all over the ice.

Jim Kinnell, Barrie, Ontario: Question for Stan, as a great scorer and play maker your earlier years were marked by a lot of penalties and then the subsequent years were followed by almost no penalties. You earned the Lady Byng as well as the Art Ross trophies back to back in '66 and '67—what was the reason for the turn around?

Stan: Well let's go back to the place where it all started. Bobby and I both came [up] in the '50s when there were 17 players on the team, 16 plus the goalie, and we only had one

Bobby Hull, arguably the best left winger in NHL history, won back-to-back Hart Trophies as league MVP in 1965 and 1966.

goalie. The problem was when I broke in I was 18 years old, I was 5'8" and weighed 152 pounds, and I was trying to make a living in a game where you have to hit people and they hit you. Well, for my first left winger I had a gentlemen by the name of Ted Lindsay—you were speaking of Gordie Howe, Teddy was my idol because he was my size and I kind of likened myself to his way of playing. I was fortunate enough to have him as my first left winger. We were sitting on the bench one day and I looked at Teddy and said, "Teddy, I'm just a little bit bigger than you. I'm 5'8" you're 5'7". I weigh a 152 pounds your about 160, how the hell do you as a fairly little guy make it to 16 years in this league?" And he looked at me and said, "Kid, hit 'em first." So I took that to be what was gospel I guess coming from him, and I wanted to belong. I wanted to play hockey and because you only had 16 players on a team they tried to test you and run you out of the league if they could. There were a lot of guys that left before I did mainly because they couldn't take it in the corners. That's why I was what I would call a tough guy.

AK: And then as time went on did you have other guys on the team that filled that role?

Stan: Well they didn't have to fill a role because the guys quit chasing me.

Bobby: Tell them why you stopped spending a lot of time in the penalty box when your daughter Meg went to the game. Stan asked his daughter Meggie on the way home how she enjoyed the game. "Well, it was okay daddy," she said. "Is that all Meggie?" "Yeah, I guess so daddy, just one question, why do all the Blackhawks sit on one side of the ice and you sit on the other by yourself?"

Stan: Bobby tells the story better than I do, she was all of what 6-years-old when she said that.

Fred Petrino, Downers Grove, IL: Bobby, one of the most famous photographs of you is the bloody one. My father told me that it was a result of a high stick from John

Ferguson. What was the rivalry or even the feud between you and him in the '60s?

Bobby: His father was absolutely right. I got clipped in the nose, actualy it was as much my fault as it was Ferguson's, but when I saw who it was, that it was his stick that clipped me, I took exception to it because of the type of person he was and we dropped our sticks and gloves and threw a few punches at one another and it was just because it was Ferguson. Had it been anyone else, it would have passed and I wouldn't have cared. It looked worse than what it was. It just knocked the skin off of my nose and it bled kind of profusely and on a white jersey you could see the blood.

Joe Simanis, Wilmette, IL: Did Bobby and Stan really invent the curved stick and how did it happen?

Bobby: Stan invented it.

Stan: Well, I have been accused of a lot of things, but unfortunately I get the blame for coming out with the curved stick. There is only one guy that is living today who thinks differently and that is Andy Bathgate and he thought that I stole the idea from him. The story goes that we went to New York to play, we usually carried three sticks each for the game and they were being shipped there and somehow or another, my three sticks got lost somewhere. So I asked their trainer, who I think was Frankie Paste, if I could borrow a stick or two, but we had another game somewhere else so I didn't need three. I said that I need a right-hand shot, lies such and such, and whatever it was 6, 7. He said the only guy that fits that description is Bathgate, he's got plenty of sticks so here take three. So I picked out three and took them. I never noticed a curve on them if there was one, but forty years later Andy was talking to a newspaper guy and kind of put a buzz in his ear and next thing you know it's in the paper that Bathgate actually invented the curved stick. It was like all great inventions—it was by accident. We had a scrimmage during practice and somebody knocked me into the boards right where the gate opens and there was about

a half-inch opening between two pieces of wood, one that would open and one that was stationary and my stick went in there right and at the same time someone hit me from the back as I was going forward. I still had my stick in my hand and I heard a crunch and I knew it was not my ribs or anything, and as it turned out the play stopped and my stick got stuck in this doorway. So finally I get it out and it was actually bent in the shape of the letter "L" and the back of it was laminated, so it only cracked; it didn't break though—and that was the origin of the curved hockey stick.

Bobby: Bathgate claims that when he was playing junior hockey in Ontario he put a hook in his blade and he happened to fire one over the glass, or over the chicken wire at that time, struck a lady in the head and cut her quite badly, and from then on his coach Alfie Pike said, "Bathgate there will be no more hooks in your stick because we are going to have a lawsuit on our hands." Andy claims he was the first

guy to use that hook back then.

Stan: This is the first time that I am hearing this story. So how long ago was that one Bobby?

Bobby: Well this has got to be when Andy was in junior hockey and he is a heck of a lot older than you and I.

Stan: Of course, at least two years.

Bobby: So this would have been early '50s I would expect, early to middle '50s when Andy played for the Guelph Biltmores.

Barry Clinton, Warminster, PA: With so many great players in Chicago back in the '60s, how come the Blackhawks didn't win a handful of Stanley Cups during that decade?

Stan: Well, if you hit a goal post or if you hit the cross bar the puck doesn't go in usually, sometimes it does and that happened to us a couple of times and the gentleman sitting on my left happened to be one of them. It was the

"Stosh" played his entire 22-year NHL career with the Blackhawks and was part of the 1961 Stanley Cup team, which he led in scoring throughout the playoffs.

seventh game in the Chicago Stadium and the second period we had a 2–0 lead against Montreal. Bobby picks up the puck behind our own net and with his usual flair picks up a little steam a little more steam and so on, and so by the time he hits the red line, he's going at full tilt. Both benches are standing and the entire stadium is standing and from the blue line and the puck, I don't know exactly what happened to it but I heard a clink and then a clank and thought, "My God, what was that?" Well, Bobby had hit the cross bar and the same puck hit the goal post and then went out. In this very same play, a continuation of it, Jacques Laperrier gets the puck, threw it up the middle to Jacques Lemaire and the rest is history. We know what Lemaire did, threw a knuckler and Tony Espostio I think was in the nets and Tony never saw it because the puck dropped a good foot, foot and a half and made it 2–1 instead of the 3–0 that could have happened ten seconds earlier. That was the ball game because of the momentum it gave to the Montreal Canadiens, and that was just one game. We had four or five other times that we were in the finals that we just couldn't get over that hump. In '65–'66 we got beat by a goaltender who the night before we scored 11 on him and they were sending for another goalie and the guy couldn't get in because of the snow and they had to play the same guy—he stopped everything but that old kitchen sink, and they beat us 3–1, I believe.

Bobby: In '67, we won the league championship by a landslide—then we hit Toronto and we hit two hot goaltenders Johnny Bower and Terry Sawchuk and we couldn't put anything past them and they beat us here 2–1, right here in Chicago.

David Muise, Yarmouth, Nova Scotia: Besides you guys, who do you think would help this present team the most, that is who was a teammate of yours?

Stan: I don't know. I haven't seen the current Blackhawks that much to be able to tell you. I think some of these young kids have all of the talent possible and just looking at them, not really talking to them yet, I can see where they could fit in with a lot of people—that is what makes a competitive and a good scoring line and a good defensive line.

Bobby: I wouldn't doubt that they could always stand strength up the middle and give them Tony Esposito or Glenn Hall and then Pierre Pilote, Billy White and Pat Stapleton. They would fit in real well with this team. They just need a few seasoned guys to help the kids out.

Perry Zavitz, Vancouver, BC: Do you two share the excitement about the present Hawk team and where they are going and do you see any see any similarities between the Hull/Mikita and the Toews/Kane pairings?

Stan: Well I don't think I've seen the Bobby Hull yet on the current team but like I have said I haven't been watching them that much. Bobby's forte was picking up the puck and bringing the crowd out of their seats as he proceeded down the ice and with each stride he would pick up a little more steam. What made this great was when they caught on to what he was trying to do. They double-teamed him and all he did was throw it away to another one of our teammates, because these guys would remain open, and that's what made him so tough. The biggest thing was Bobby's slap shot. Don't talk to me about his slap shot; ask some of those goaltenders who he was facing.

AK: Bobby, Jonathan Toews is someone the fans really see maybe in that Stan Mikita role. I know those are big words, but do you see him as a guy who plays with that kind of toughness and that kind of skill?

Bobby: Pound for pound Stan was the greatest player that ever played and Jonathan Toews or Patrick Kane have a long way to go to catch up to Mr. Mikita.

Stan: But they will be there. ●

Bobby Hull registered his first 50-goal season in 1965–66, when he also became the first player in NHL history to surpass 50 goals in a season. He scored his 51st goal against the Rangers' Cesare Maniago on March 12, 1966.

Fan Q&A with Tony Esposito

HawkCast, the Official Blackhawks Podcast, March 19, 2008

William Cotton from Tinley Park, IL: How does it feel to be a part of the Chicago Blackhawks organization again, and do you know how much it means to Chicago Blackhawks fans to know that you are back?

Tony: First of all, I am thankful that they are happy to see me back. Secondly, when I was done playing, things happened and unfortunately I wasn't involved with the team for a number of years, and it's not my doing it just happened that way, and I am so fortunate to be back and involved. And the way we have been treated—Bobby, Stan, and I—it is just wonderful. Rocky Wirtz and John McDonough just welcomed us into the family and I am excited about it and hope it goes on for a long time.

Tony Orona from Chicago: When playing in your first game, how was it that your brother [Phil] was the first one to score on you?

Tony: He not only scored the first one, he scored the second one. The score was 2–2 and he got them both. He sure got heck from my mother, I tell ya. Oh, she was angry!

Don Milliak: Who was the toughest shooter to face on a breakaway besides your brother?

Tony: I would have to say maybe Guy Lafleur was one of the toughest, he was tricky. The guys that were fast were really tough. Mike Bossy was a problem because he was tricky around the net.

Darcy from Thunder Bay, Ontario: Of all years that you played, what defensemen that you played behind was the most reliable/underrated?

Tony: Well my opinion, Doug Wilson was the best defensemen we ever had, overall defenseman; but the best defensive defenseman was Bill White by far.

Charles Kenville from Des Moines, Iowa: How does goaltending coaching and development in today's game compare to when you were an up-and-coming goalie? Were there goaltending camps and clinics, or did you have to figure things out for yourself? How did you develop your style?

Tony: Well, I had no goalie coach—it was unheard of in those days. We were lucky to have a backup goaltender let alone a goalie coach. Secondly, I learned how to play basically myself through observation, and I stole things from older goalies. I brought in some stuff from Glenn Hall, I used a little bit of his style because I played a lot like him. Johnny Bower, I picked the poke check from him, and I picked the meanness and the desire from Terry Sawchuk. Putting that all together and combining.

Stan Ketcik from Minooka, IL: You left our city but never our hearts, you were a goaltending innovator each year building more padding and protection to your mask and equipment. Compare the equipment today to what was available when you played.

During his 15-year tenure with the Blackhawks, Tony Esposito won three Vezina Trophies as the NHL's best goaltender. He still holds the team's career shutout record (74).

Tony: Well first of all, I should have patented a lot of those things because they have employed them now. The equipment is a lot better, a lot lighter, so it really adds better protection and the weight, like I said, gives you longevity. The way the face masks are today you don't really get hurt ever. Except for unforeseen knee injury if a guy falls on you, you can play a long time. It is a combination of things how they protect the goalie. The backup goalie plays quite a bit now. The travel is so much easier with the charters and stuff.

Matt Foy from Hoffman Estates, IL: Tony is it true in a game you wore a net between the legs to close up the five hole? What other tricks did you have up your sleeve when you played?

Tony: Well, I used that for a year or two and after they happened to notice it they put a rule in and that was the end of that. I've done a lot of things—you know how the

catching glove is with that mesh on that side? I used fabric on there, same idea. I was the founder of the neck piece and a few other things.

Eileen Darin from Crest Hill, IL: How do you think the style has changed since you were a player? Is it faster, slower, more aggressive, less aggressive?

Tony: Well, what I would like her to do is look at that hockey game that is going to be on tomorrow. It is on tonight at 10:30 and tomorrow morning. You'll see the style—the referee didn't call as many penalties, and they allowed you to play more so they allowed more physical [contact]. The game has changed because of these rules. It is helping a lot [of] the smaller players these days. It allows the smaller players to excel more because they don't get beat up as much. When we had a young kid come in the old days they used to run them to death, especially if he was a smaller

Esposito is the Blackhawks' career leader in wins (418) and ranks seventh all-time in NHL history with 423 wins.

guy—so that is why they didn't come in as young. I think the rules are good for that to help develop youth.

John Janota from Joliet: How do you feel about the rule changes for goaltenders in the last few years? Do you like them, dislike them, think they are fair, unfair?

Tony: Well I don't think that it has hurt them at all. They haven't cut the size of the equipment down, so that is one good thing. Another thing is that they have that big crease it is a lot bigger than it was in the old days. The only thing is they can't wander as much behind the net but I don't think it's affecting them that much. I think the rule changes have benefited them a lot.

Dale Kew from Stony Plain, Alberta: I saw a show about you a few years back, about your basement and all of the Blackhawks memorabilia you have. Do you still have all this

memorabilia and, if yes, which means the most to you?

Tony: I have all of that stuff and unfortunately I don't have a huge home as I had when I was here in north Chicago. I have an area where I put out the most important stuff. I would probably have to say my facemask is the thing I relate to the most because I wore it so much.

Jeff Reid from North Bay, Ontario: You faced Bobby Hull regularly in practice, how do you think his slap shot compares to the slap shots of today?

Tony: I still think Bobby Hull was the hardest shooter in the history of hockey. I still get to see a lot of games, and I have been involved with hockey up until 2000. I can tell by standing up at the glass how hard a guy shoots and I think he was probably just as hard a shooter as anybody ever.

Esposito, shown above with his now-famous goalie mask, was formally introduced as a Blackhawks Ambassador on March 19, 2008.

John Wagner from Deer Park, IL: Can you describe the experience and pressure of playing goal in Russia before and during game seven of the Summit Series in September 1972?

Tony: Well, when it's do-or-die there's a lot of pressure on you, so what you do is just suck it up and the good guys excel and they win it and the lesser guys crack and they fold on you. I just remember that and knew that I had to come out big and fortunately we won the game.

Brian Miller from Palos Park, IL: In 1981 you gained U.S. citizenship—was that something for yourself personally, or was that so you could play for the U.S. in the Canada Cup?

Tony: No, it was for my owner. It was for Bill Wirtz who owned the Chicago Blackhawks. He wanted me to play in

that tournament and I said, "Well, I can't play." I thought I had a way out. I said, "I'm not a citizen." And he said well there is only three weeks time before the series so I said there is no chance he can ever get my citizenship. I had my citizenship in two weeks, and I ended up having to go and play in that tournament—but it was enjoyable.

Adam Kempenaar, HawkCast Host: When thinking of Chicago Stadium, what is the first thing that comes to mind?

Tony: The roar of the crowd, I guess that is the first thing. The noise and people involved and the National Anthem, too, but it was the people, the fans, that I remember. ●

Esposito set the Blackhawks team record for shutouts in a season (15) during the 1969–70 campaign—his rookie year.

Pierre Pilote

By Harvey Wittenberg

Little did Blackhawks general manager Tommy Ivan envision in 1955 when he convinced the team owners to buy the minor league Buffalo team for $150,000 what a bargain it would turn out to be.

Ivan was lured from Detroit to turn the Hawks into a winner and break the Stanley Cup grip held by Montreal, Toronto and Detroit.

A 24-year-old defenseman, Pierre Pilote, was called up from Buffalo in February 1956 for the final 20 games and registered three goals and five assists.

Pilote went on to a fantastic career with the Blackhawks. Not only did he become the first Chicago Norris Trophy winner, awarded to the NHL's top defenseman, he won it three years in a row (1963, 1964, and 1965) – the only Hawks blueliner to achieve that feat. Pilote was named to the NHL All-Star team eight straight seasons. He was Hawks team captain for eight years (1961–68)—again the longest tenure in team history, including the year of our last Stanley Cup.

In the 1964–65 campaign, Pilote set an NHL record for most points in a season by a defenseman (59). When the Hawks won the Cup in 1961, "Pete" tied Detroit's Gordie Howe for most points in the playoffs (15), which is something considering a couple of teammates, Bobby Hull and Stan Mikita, were better known as offensive players.

In his 13 seasons with the Hawks, Pete registered 77 goals and 400 assists in 821 games. He ranks sixth among Chicago players in assists which places him second among blueliners behind Doug Wilson. Also, he is 11th in games played and 17th in total points, placing him third among Hawk defensemen.

Perhaps one of the best tributes that could be paid to Pilote came from all-time NHL great Bobby Orr, who broke Pete's record for most points in a season by a defenseman. Orr said that in some ways he copied some of Pete's offensive style while adding some of his own.

Up until the mid-1950s, NHL defensemen were expected to stay back and not get involved in the offense. Montreal's Doug Harvey was the top blueliner of his day, and he started some offense, but Pete really added to it with his skating ability, making a defenseman the fourth player on the attack.

In 1975, the NHL named Pilote along with his Cup-winning goalie, Glenn Hall, to the Hockey Hall of Fame. That honor came one year after Chicago's legendary general manager, Tommy Ivan, was inducted, and 20 years after Ivan persuaded the owners to pick up that minor league Buffalo team for $150,000 with a young defenseman named Pilote. ●

Pilote's No. 3 was retired in a ceremony November 12, 2008.

Defenseman Pierre Pilote won the Norris Trophy, awarded to the NHL's best defenseman, in three consecutive seasons (1963–65).

Pilote led the Blackhawks in scoring with 15 points during their championship run in 1961.

Keith Magnuson

By Harvey Wittenberg

Most athletes are honored for their amazing accomplishments on the field of battle, but on very rare occasions some are recognized for what they do after their playing careers have ended.

Such is the case with the late Keith Magnuson, who excelled as a tremendous person after his athletic career and whose heart and soul will forever shine as a true Blackhawk for his deeds on behalf of and his compassion toward his fellow man.

You won't find Keith's name in the Chicago record books unless you scan down to who racked up 291 penalty minutes in a season to rank 10th in Hawks history or to learn that he is second in team history in total time spent in the penalty box behind Chris Chelios.

I guess if you polled fans from other arenas in the NHL during his 11 seasons as a Hawk, they might describe him as a "dirty" player. However, to me, his teammates, and college buddies Cliff Koroll and Jim Wiste, the more appropriate description would be defender.

Magnuson was the consummate Blackhawk from the first day he wore the crest and always stuck up for his teammates. Not the fastest or most skilled competitor, Magnuson always gave more than 100 percent, which continued on after his career. He played a major role in helping others in his post as president of the Blackhawk Alumni Association, promoting amateur hockey and the Hawks up until the day of his untimely death.

When Magnuson joined the team in 1969 after being captain of the NCAA Champion University of Denver team,
he wasn't even signed to a contract and his agent was at odds with general manager Tommy Ivan.

Hawks coach Billy Reay was more inclined to play veterans and didn't like the thought of using a lot of rookies especially coming in a season after the Hawks finished last. But with the likes of Maggie playing, the team went from worst to first for the only time in NHL history.

A deal was struck and in Maggie's first preseason game against Montreal at the Stadium, the rookie leveled Canadiens' tough guy John Ferguson over the boards and the Magnuson/Hawks love affair began.

Maggie didn't score a goal that season but set a team record for penalty box time—213 minutes!

While the statistics show he wasn't a goal scorer, on April 11, 1975, in the playoffs in Boston, he opened the scoring to help the Hawks upset the Bobby Orr-led Bruins. Maggie was the Hawks' captain for three seasons (1976–79) before an injury ended his career. Bob Pulford asked him to become an assistant coach and he was elevated to head coach from 1980 through January 1982, when he decided to step down.

From that point on, Keith continued to devote his efforts as a goodwill ambassador for the Hawks while spearheading efforts for high school hockey players to get college scholarships and assisting Blackhawks charities—a true humanitarian! ●

Magnuson's No. 3 was retired in a ceremony November 12, 2008.

Defenseman Keith Magnuson held the title of Blackhawks team captain from 1976 through 1979 and was immediately named an assistant head coach following his retirement.

Magnuson was known as one of the toughest Blackhawks ever, and one who would never back down from a fight.

Glenn Hall

By Harvey Wittenberg

Can any goalie imagine playing today in the NHL without a mask? Hall of Fame goalie Glenn Hall patrolled the Blackhawk nets for 10 seasons while leading them to the 1961 Stanley Cup—and did it all without facial protection. Besides being named to 13 NHL All-Star Games, Hall's record of appearing in 503-straight games is a mark that may last the longest in pro sports history. Hall was inducted into the Hockey Hall of Fame in 1975, along with teammate Pierre Pilote.

The late Hawks GM Tommy Ivan engineered one of the greatest trades in Chicago history by getting Hall from the Red Wings in 1957—the season that rookie Bobby Hull broke in with the Blackhawks. Hall won Rookie of the Year honors in 1956 and had played in 140-straight games with

Detroit before joining the Hawks. His amazing record-breaking consecutive streak continued for 363 games in Chicago until a sore back sidelined him in November 1962. Hall recorded 275 wins and 51 shutouts with the Hawks in regular-season play. When NHL expansion began in 1967 and teams could only protect one goalie, the St. Louis Blues, coached by current Hawks Senior Advisor Scotty Bowman, grabbed the All-Star. Hall went on to wind up his career with 407 wins and 84 shutouts, which ranks him among the top 10 in league history.

Hall won the Vezina Trophy as the league's top goalie on three different occasions, twice with the Blackhawks. When the NHL came out with its All-Century Team, he was ranked second. Scotty Bowman observed that while the late Terry Sawchuk was listed as No. 1, Sawchuk had the advantages of stronger defensemen in front of him.

When Hall was snatched by the Blues, he finally donned a mask and played with another future Hall of Famer, Jacques Plante, who was the first NHL goalie to adopt wearing a mask full-time.

Naturally, Hall was named to the Hawks' 75th Anniversary All-Star team. His No. 1 jersey was fittingly retired in 1988 at the United Center along with another all-time-great Blackhawks goalie, Tony Esposito. ●

The Blackhawks will honor Glenn Hall with a Heritage Night celebration on April 1, 2009.

Goaltender Glenn Hall played in a then-NHL record 503 consecutive games—all without the protection of a face mask.

(L-R): Bobby Hull, Stan Mikita, Bill Hay, and Glenn Hall were part of the 1961 Stanley Cup Championship team.

The MPH Line

One of the most prolific lines in Blackhawks history, the "MPH Line"—comprised of Pit Martin, Jim Pappin, and Dennis Hull—personified teamwork and excellence in the late 1960s and early 1970s. In an era where line combinations were shuffled regularly, the trio played together for seven years and produced more than 1,300 points.

What's ironic about one of the greatest lines in Hawks history is that they were never supposed to play together: both Pappin and Martin were brought to Chicago to play alongside Dennis' brother, Bobby. But after "The Golden Jet" held out due to a contract dispute before the 1969–70 season, the MPH Line found such great success that no coach in his right mind could tear them apart.

"Bobby didn't need anyone specific to play with," says Pappin. "He would score 50 goals when he played with me and he would score 50 goals if he played with someone else."

Once the line came together, they became a dominating offensive force. In those days, when teams were only expected to have two offensively minded lines with the third line focused on defense, the Hawks were blessed with three groups of goal-scorers.

"We always figured that Stan Mikita was on the first line and Bobby was on the second," says Martin. "We ended up with three really good lines."

While Bobby and Stan grabbed the headlines, the Hawks' "checking line" of Martin, Pappin, and Hull registered a then-team record for points in a season by a line (272 in 1972–73) and were major contributors in two Stanley Cup Finals appearances (1971 and 1973).

"We fooled a lot of teams; they thought we were only a defensive line. Maybe that's why we scored so many goals," jokes Hull. "The third line may only score 15 or 20 goals these days; we scored 100."

But what defines the MPH Line more than anything is their sense of brotherhood and duty to one another. Not only were the three linemates for seven seasons, but they were also roommates on the road and if they weren't with their wives, they were with each other.

"I was always happier when Pit and Jimmy scored than when I did," says Hull. "I'm sure they felt the same."

That teammate-first attitude is embodied best in Martin's favorite story from his playing days, when during a fast break Pappin passed him the puck then threw away his stick.

"Jimmy threw his stick away because he knew I'd give [the puck] back to him," he explains. "He didn't want me to give it back; he wanted me to score."

Not that it would've mattered much.

"I was ready," says Pappin, who fondly recalls the moment. "If he would've passed it back to me, I would've passed it right back." ●

The Blackhawks will honor the MPH Line with a Heritage Night celebration on March 11, 2009.

The "MPH Line" of (top to bottom) Pit Martin, Jim Pappin, and Dennis Hull played together for seven seasons and amassed more than 1,300 points as a line.

Steve Larmer

By Harvey Wittenberg

For those of you who have had the fortune through the years to see the many spectacular plays by Chicago greats Bobby Hull, Stan Mikita, Denis Savard, Jeremy Roenick, and Bill Mosienko, I want to add the best two-way Hawks player I have had the pleasure of witnessing—Steve Larmer.

Not to diminish the defensive prowess of the aforementioned Hawks, but Larmer—perhaps the greatest draft steal in franchise history (sixth round in 1980)—did the job game in and game out in what might be called "non-spectacular" fashion!

Larmer played in 866 consecutive games in his 13 seasons (1982–1993). After brief stints with the Hawks in 1980-81 and 1981–82 while mainly playing for the team's AHL affiliate, Larmer won Rookie of the Year honors in 1983 after amassing 43 goals and 47 assists to total 90 points. Larmer played on a line with Denis Savard and Al Secord that amassed 297 points—also still a team mark.

Larmer went on to accumulate 406 goals with 517 assists for a total of 923 points, ranking him third, fifth, and fourth in team history, respectively. Larmer also registered five 40-plus goal seasons and achieved a remarkable 101 point total in 1990–91.

During his career he played both on the power play and penalty kill. Ironically, he is the highest scoring right winger in Hawks annals with a left-hand shot. Larmer, known by his teammates as "Gramps," also ranks fourth on the team in playoff goals and assists.

He had nine hat tricks, fourth most in team history, and possesses the fastest overtime goal (eight seconds), against Washington in October 1990.

He was a member of the Hawks squad that captured the President's Trophy with 106 points in 1992–93 for the most points in the NHL.

Quiet and unassuming, Larmer shares a number of records with the likes of Hull, Mikita, and Savard, including scoring in six straight playoff games and most points in a playoff game (five).

Recognized by Chicago fans, he was named to the Blackhawks 75th Anniversary All-Star Team as one of the top three right wings. Although he was never voted to the NHL All-Star team, his outstanding play should earn him his rightful place in the Hockey Hall of Fame.

Again, while he may not have appeared spectacular to some, Larmer's stats prove he always got the job done! ●

The Blackhawks will honor Steve Larmer with a Heritage Night celebration on December 3, 2008.

Steve Larmer caught the attention of Hawks fans from the word "go," scoring 90 points (43 goals, 47 assists) his rookie season and winning the 1983 Calder Trophy.

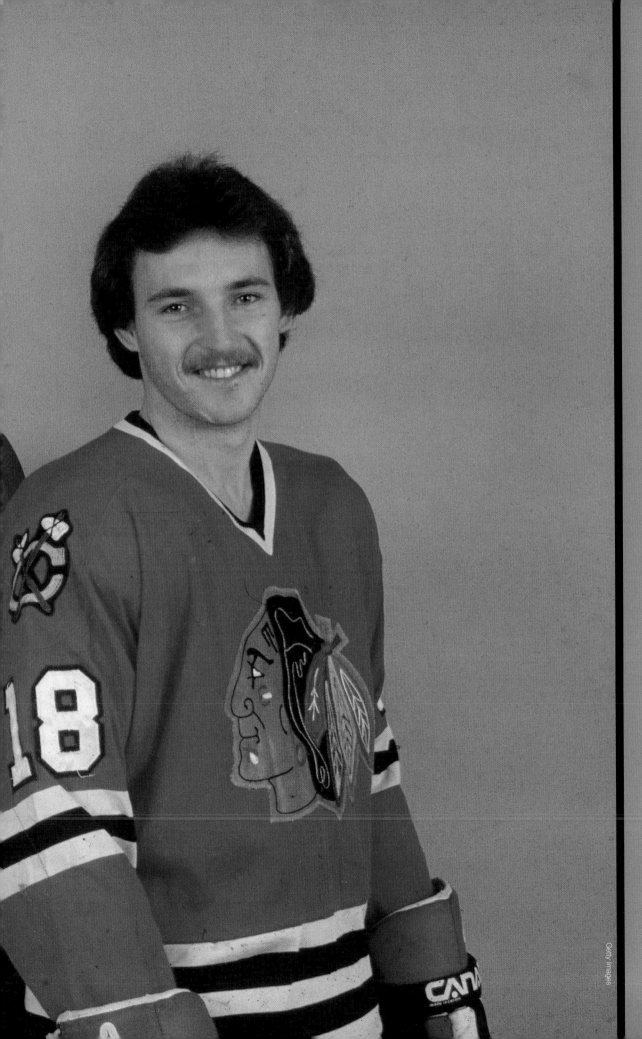

Larmer (28) teamed with Al Secord (20) and Denis Savard (18) to form the "Party Line" during the 1980s. The trio still holds the team record for points by a line in a season.

Bob Probert

Best known as a fighter and enforcer, forward Bob Probert finished his career fourth on the NHL all-time list with 3,300 penalty minutes in 16 NHL seasons. Perhaps not surprisingly, former Blackhawks teammates such as television analyst Eddie Olczyk always wanted to stay on Probert's good side.

"I would much rather play with him than against him," said Olczyk, who played against him during Probert's stint with the Red Wings from 1984–87 and with him on the Hawks from 1998–2000. "Whenever you saw the whites of Probie's eyes you better get the hell out of the way. Probie just had that presence, everybody felt a little bigger and a little tougher when he was there in the lineup. The game has changed a lot, but Probie was always there for his teammates. I don't know if he got all the credit for that."

Probert appeared in 935 regular season NHL contests, posting 163 goals and 221 assists for 384 points. In 81 post-season games, Probert registered 16 goals, 32 assists and 274 penalty minutes.

Probert began his Blackhawks' career when he signed as a free agent, July 23, 1994. The Windsor, Ontario, native spent seven seasons with the club, where he appeared in 461 regular-season contests.

Olczyk remembers Probert as one of the toughest players ever in the National Hockey League.

"He's certainly got to be one of the top [enforcers] ever," said Olczyk. "When you think back to the early '70s you go back to Dave Schultz and Terry O'Reilly, and he's got to be in the top 10 for sure.... He was tough. He could give them and he could take them, too. A lot of guys are tough and they can't take one, but he has taken a handful for sure."

While with Chicago, he recorded 49 goals, 76 assists, and 1,210 penalty minutes until he officially announced his retirement November 16, 2002. Probert ranked first on the team in penalty minutes during the 1995–96, 1996–97, 1998–99 and 2001–02 seasons. He also currently ranks 42nd on the Blackhawks lifetime leaders list for games played. ●

The Blackhawks will honor Bob Probert with a Heritage Night celebration on February 22, 2009.

Signed from the Detroit Red Wings before the 1994–95 season, Bob Probert became the physical force for the Blackhawks in the late '90s, leading the team in penalty minutes four times.

One of the league's all-time great enforcers, Bob Probert accrued 1,210 penalty minutes in 461 games with Chicago.

Tony Amonte

By Harvey Wittenberg

Tony Amonte was a popular, speedy right wing who joined the Hawks in March 1994 after a trade with the Rangers. He appeared in five straight All-Star Games from 1997 through 2001 and was selected as one of the three right wingers on Chicago's 75th Anniversary Team.

Amonte scored the first hat trick in the new United Center on February 22, 1996, against St. Louis—the first of six in his Blackhawk career, which ties him for seventh with Hawks Al Secord and Jeremy Roenick.

Amonte led the team in scoring for four straight years (1996–2000) and his two-season total of 87 (1998–2000) was tops in the NHL. He became the 13th player in Hawks history to score 40-plus goals, which he did three times. Amonte enjoyed six-straight seasons of 30-plus goals and also established himself as a fixture on the ice for the Blackhawks, missing only one game between 1996 and 2002.

Amonte was team captain from 2000–2002 and compiled a Hawks career total in regular season play of 268 goals (sixth all-time) and 541 total points, good for the ninth spot among Chicago players in his nine campaigns in the Windy City.

The Hingham, Massachusetts, native represented the United States in both the 1998 and 2002 Winter Olympics. Amonte played at Thayer Academy, where he was a teammate of Roenick's. They were reunited with the Hawks from the time Amonte joined the team in 1994 through the 1995–96 season. Originally drafted by the Rangers, Amonte played in the NHL Rookie All-Star game in 1992 and was selected by *The Hockey News* as the Rookie of the Year.

In his brilliant NHL career, Amonte amassed 900 points in 1,174 games; he recorded another 22 goals and 55 points in the playoffs. ●

The Blackhawks will honor Tony Amonte with a Heritage Night celebration on January 21, 2009

In his nine-year career with the Chicago Blackhawks, Tony Amonte scored 268 goals and netted 30 or more goals six times.

Amonte currently ranks eleventh all-time in points among American-born players (900).

Cam Barker

#	Player	Height	Weight	DOB	Age	Birthplace
25	Cam Barker	6'3"	213	April 4, 1986	22	Winnipeg, MB, CAN

Sometimes it takes a bit of time to succeed in the NHL, even if you were one of the top picks in your draft class. Defenseman Cam Barker can attest to that. As the third pick in 2004 (Alex Ovechkin and Evgeny Malkin were first and second, respectively), Barker has taken a few seasons to reach the Blackhawks as a full-time contributor, but he says it's all for the better.

"I'm still young," says Barker. "It takes a while to really step in and find your niche. I want to be good every night and I want to be good right away."

Last season, Barker spent the majority of the season (45 games) in the NHL for the first time in his career, and he responded by tallying 18 points and playing solid defense. After being recalled by the Blackhawks in late October this year, Barker has returned to form as the team's up-and-coming two-way defenseman.

"He has a lot of talent," says fellow blueliner Brian Campbell. "He's still learning and he's going to find ways to get better. It's tough to remember he's only 22. He still needs people to help him and work with him, but he has the work ethic to do it."

Barker knows that reaching the professional ranks is only half the battle; staying there is what's most important. As he keeps developing, hard work and perseverance will ultimately be the keys to his success.

"The more time goes by I need to keep playing well and stay focused," he says. "I'm just trying to get better every day. I know I'm ready." ●

Defenseman Cam Barker recorded NHL career highs in games (45), goals (6), assists (12), points (18), and penalty minutes (52) with the Blackhawks in 2007–08.

Dave Bolland

#	Player	Height	Weight	DOB	Age	Birthplace
36	Dave Bolland	6' 0"	181	June 5, 1986	22	Mimico, ON, CAN

Just a hair over 6', if that, Dave Bolland has often heard that he's too small to be an effective player in the NHL. Fortunately for the Blackhawks, he's got a big game.

"Some people have told me that I was a little on the small side," said Bolland. "I take that to my advantage. The

way I play is bigger than I am; I just take that negativity out with me on the ice."

Bolland's play has stood out to head coach Joel Quenneville, who has given Bolland time on both the Blackhawks' power-play and penalty-killing units, trusting him in the most important moments of a game.

"[Playing special teams] means that I have a lot of responsibility, that the coaches think that I can play in those situations," said Bolland. "It shows they respect my game."

Bolland, the Hawks' second choice in the 2004 NHL Entry Draft, is part of the Hawks' youth movement, which has seen players like Dustin Byfuglien, Duncan Keith, James Wisniewski, and others make the jump from the AHL to the NHL. Bolland showed he deserved a spot on the Hawks roster with several spot appearances with the parent club last season when he scored 17 points (4 goals, 13 assists) in 39 games.

"All of these young guys are hungry and they want to play," said Bolland of his teammates. "It feels good to see all of these young guys out there and I think overall we've been playing well together."

If Bolland continues to play his game, the Hawks will see the small player come up big. ●

Despite his lack of NHL experience, head coach Joel Quenneville has entrusted Dave Bolland with a spot on both the power-play and penalty-killing units.

Adam Burish

#	Player	Height	Weight	DOB	Age	Birthplace
37	Adam Burish	6' 1"	189	Jan 6, 1983	25	Madison, WI, USA

Call Adam Burish what you will; he has many labels. He's an instigator. A talker. An enforcer. A winner. "I go out there and I like to mix it up. I like confrontation," says Burish, the Blackhawks' reigning penalty minutes champion and the odds-on favorite to repeat the title this season.

Burish distinguished himself in four years at the University of Wisconsin, where he captained the 2006 NCAA

championship team. But to make it in the NHL, he's had to transform his game from simply being the physical player that he was in Madison to the agitator who racked up 24 penalty minutes in one game last January.

"The biggest thing for me is that I love sticking up for my teammates," says Burish, proud of the number of hits he's dished out and received along the way. "The respect that you get from the guys on the bench when you do something like that—it's something special."

He has a knack for talking as well; Burish could teach a master's class on a subject he knows nothing about and you'd hang on his every word. In the locker room, it's a welcome distraction; for opposing players, it's a dangerous game.

"I love the look on some guys' faces when you can see you're in their kitchen," explained Burish. "I love taking the opportunity when I get out there to say 'you're not getting in Kane or Toews' face. I'm not going to let you. If you do that, I'm going to hold you accountable.'"

And if someone crosses the line Burish knows what to do there, too.

"Fighting's just a rush of excitement," he says. "Sometimes you go out there looking for it, sometimes it just happens. But you look at the other guy and he gives you a nod and you give him a nod...it's just a rush of adrenaline." ●

By playing his tough, physical game, combined with his love of talking trash, Adam Burish garnered a team-high 214 penalty minutes in 2007–08.

Dustin Byfuglien

#	PLAYER	HEIGHT	WEIGHT	DOB	AGE	BIRTHPLACE
33	DUSTIN BYFUGLIEN	6'3"	247	MARCH 27, 1985	23	MINNEAPOLIS, MN, USA

Dustin Byfuglien isn't the loudest player in the Blackhawks' locker room. But "Buff" doesn't have to score the highlight reel goals. His tough, gritty play on the ice speaks for itself every game.

"I just do what I know can do," says Byfuglien. "Whether it's offense or playing defense, I do whatever I can. I know my role."

Byfuglien's role in 2007–08 resulted in arguably the biggest breakout season by a Hawk not named Kane, Toews, or Sharp. An eighth-round 2003 Entry Draft pick, Byfuglien netted 19 goals and registered 59 penalty minutes in 67 games after only scoring 8 points in 34 career NHL games previously. He recorded one of only two Blackhawks hat tricks of the season on November 30 against Phoenix.

His improvement on offense led the Blackhawks coaching staff to move Byfuglien from his natural position on defense to forward.

"I feel like the transition has gone well so far," he says. "Sometimes you have to find ways to keep improving and to stay out of prolonged slumps. I think I've been alright so far."

Byfuglien knows playing forward at a high level will take time to learn, but he's committed to playing wherever the team needs him.

"My goal is to compete and battle every shift," says Byfuglien. "I have to be more consistent on offense to be effective for the team." ●

Seeing his first regular NHL action, Byfuglien scored 36 points (19 goals, 17 assists) in 67 games last season, prompting a position change from defense to forward.

Though he no longer patrols the blue line, "Buff" still provides a physical presence for the Hawks.

Martin Havlat

#	PLAYER	HEIGHT	WEIGHT	DOB	AGE	BIRTHPLACE
24	MARTIN HAVLAT	6' 2"	217	APRIL 19, 1981	27	MLADA BOLESLAV, CZE

The Blackhawks knew exactly what they were getting when they traded for winger Martin Havlat in 2006. A proven goal scorer in five seasons with Ottawa, Havlat is best known for his offensive intensity and highlight-reel goals.

"He's a top guy and I think he can be the difference-maker on a lot of nights," says Blackhawks head coach Joel Quenneville. "Top guys like that you want to enhance their creativity and support that in a lot of areas. We expect our top guys to lead in a number of ways, and he's one of them."

Since his first NHL game in 2000, Havlat's been a force of nature; in 389 games through the 2007–08 season, Havlat has 319 points (140 goals, 179 assists) and a career plus/minus of 58.

Havlat has been a tremendous athlete, but his health has been a concern throughout his career. He played in just 35 games in 2007–08 after shoulder surgery ended his season. He really was never totally healthy, but still managed to produce 10 goals and 17 assists with one good shoulder.

Although watching from the sidelines was hard for him, Havlat says that he's back and feeling good after rehabilitation all off-season.

"I'm starting the year healthy, and that's what I was working for the whole summer," says Havlat. "Last year was tough, but I feel pretty good right now."

Feeling 100 percent again, Havlat can go back to making plays the way that only he can. With any luck, there will be many more highlight reels in his future. ●

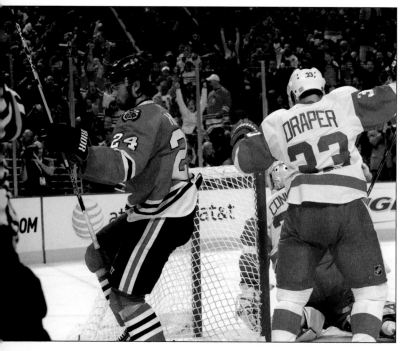

Best known for his uncanny scoring touch, Martin Havlat is one of the Hawks' most dangerous offensive threats whenever he takes the ice.

Despite appearing in just 56 games due to injury in 2006–07, his first year with the Hawks, Havlat led the team in goals (25), assists (32), and points (57).

Duncan Keith

#	PLAYER	HEIGHT	WEIGHT	DOB	AGE	BIRTHPLACE
2	DUNCAN KEITH "A"	6'1"	194	JULY 16, 1983	25	WINNIPEG, MB, CAN

When Duncan Keith was drafted by the Hawks out of Michigan State University in 2002, he was a lightweight by NHL defenseman standards at 5'11" and 168 pounds. It's hard to picture that Keith when you see the 6'1", 194-pound All-Star that he's become.

"Part of it was just maturing physically," explains Keith. "At 18 you're still a young kid, and for me it was still about the natural process of filling out. I worked in the gym and built muscle on top of that natural process. I enjoy working out and I think that helped, too."

Keith led the Blackhawks in plus/minus in 2007–08 (+30) and added 32 points (12 goals, 20 assists). He says that his biggest thrill in hockey is being a solid two-way defenseman, going one on one with an opposing team's best forward and helping his team score.

"It's tough to say what exactly [my role is on the team]," says Keith. "I love the challenge of competing against a team's best guys, playing good defense, and I can be solid offensively. I look at guys like [Detroit's] Niklas Lindstrom, a well-rounded defenseman, and that's what I try to be."

A clear sign that he's succeeding in that effort, Keith was honored by his peers and hockey fans last year when he was named to the NHL's All-Star Game.

"It was a big honor for me to play in the All-Star Game and to be considered among the NHL's best," said Keith. "There were a lot of guys who were having good years and deserved to be there as well; that made it an even bigger honor for me."

From 168-pound prospect to All-Star, Keith's grown in more ways than one. ●

Duncan Keith has transformed from a 168-pound defensive prospect into a Western Conference All-Star and the workhorse of the Blackhawks' blue line.

Keith led the Hawks
in plus/minus rating
(+30) last season,
good for second-best
in the league.

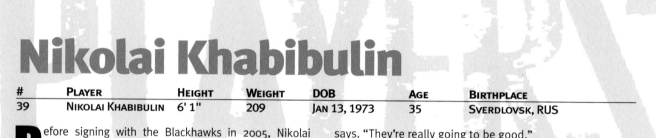

Nikolai Khabibulin

#	PLAYER	HEIGHT	WEIGHT	DOB	AGE	BIRTHPLACE
39	Nikolai Khabibulin	6' 1"	209	Jan 13, 1973	35	Sverdlovsk, RUS

Before signing with the Blackhawks in 2005, Nikolai Khabibulin brought the Tampa Bay Lightning to the championship. On a team where most players have only heard of the playoffs, having a goalie who has hoisted the Stanley Cup is a luxury the Blackhawks are fortunate to have.

"This team is a lot stronger than it was in the past, especially if you compare it to my first year," Khabibulin says. "They're really going to be good."

In 50 games with the Hawks last season, Khabibulin statistically had his best year since signing with Chicago, earning 23 wins and allowing 2.63 goals per game. Khabibulin also registered two shutouts.

"I think Nik's a great goalie," says fellow goaltender Cristobal Huet. "It's great working with him."

Khabibulin approaches every game as its own unique challenge to overcome. For a goaltender closing in on 300 career wins, his competitive spirit is the same as it was when he was a rookie in the league.

"Every year's a challenge, and every game's a challenge," says Khabibulin. "I've just got to be ready when it's my turn to play and do the best that I can."

And with any luck, Khabibulin will have the opportunity to revisit the postseason, a place he has never been with the Hawks.

"Whenever I get a chance to get in there, I'll do the best I can to help the team win and make the playoffs," says Khabibulin. ●

One of three Blackhawks with a Stanley Cup ring, Khabibulin has been a mainstay in the Blackhawks' crease since he came to the team in 2005.

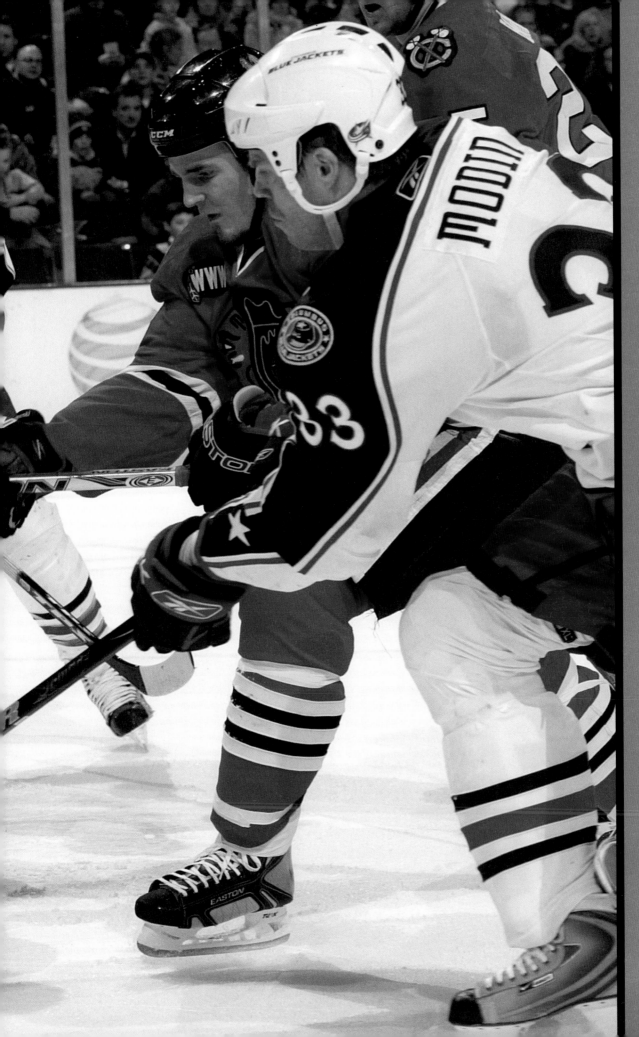

"Every year's a challenge and every game's a challenge," Khabibulin says. "I'll do the best I can to help the team win."

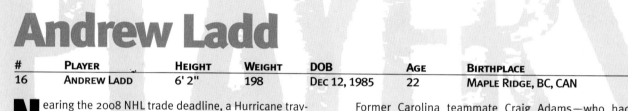

Andrew Ladd

#	PLAYER	HEIGHT	WEIGHT	DOB	AGE	BIRTHPLACE
16	ANDREW LADD	6' 2"	198	DEC 12, 1985	22	MAPLE RIDGE, BC, CAN

Nearing the 2008 NHL trade deadline, a Hurricane traveled farther west than normal: one touched down in Chicago in the form of winger Andrew Ladd. By acquiring Ladd for forward Tuomo Ruutu last February, the Blackhawks grabbed one only three players on the current squad with Stanley Cup experience—Ladd was part of the Carolina Hurricanes team that won the Cup in 2006.

Former Carolina teammate Craig Adams—who had been traded to Chicago a month before—and the welcoming atmosphere of the Blackhawks' locker room immediately made Ladd feel at home with his new team.

"Obviously, I knew Craig from Carolina, and that made the transition a little easier," says Ladd. "But overall my move to the Hawks was pretty effortless. They're a great group of talented, young guys."

On the ice, Ladd's steadily improving game has helped the Hawks on both ends of the ice. He has picked up where he left off last season, when he scored 12 points (5 goals, 7 assists) in 20 games with the Hawks.

"I think I do a little bit of everything," says Ladd. "I can be strong defensively, play a physical game, and contribute on offense, too."

With one championship ring already in his possession, Ladd sees many similarities between his current club and his Cup-raising Carolina team.

"We were an up-tempo group and played hard every day," says Ladd. "This group plays that same determined style." ●

Ladd has proven to be a force on both ends of the ice: in 63 NHL games last season, he registered 30 points (14 goals, 16 assists) and a plus/minus rating of +13.

Brent Seabrook

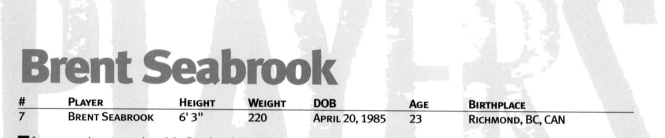

#	PLAYER	HEIGHT	WEIGHT	DOB	AGE	BIRTHPLACE
7	BRENT SEABROOK	6'3"	220	APRIL 20, 1985	23	RICHMOND, BC, CAN

If any one player can chronicle first-hand the resurgence of the Chicago Blackhawks, defenseman Brent Seabrook is the guy. Even though he has just three previous seasons of NHL hockey to his credit, he's one of the longest-tenured Blackhawks and has seen the team revitalized right before his eyes.

"It's been cool to see and obviously great to be a part

of," Seabrook says. "It's a fantastic hockey city and a great organization. It's great to see the fans come back and support us again."

Seabrook has been a consistent producer since he first entered the league, registering 56 points (9 goals, 47 assists) between 2005 and 2007. Despite his best efforts, the Hawks had just 57 wins against 85 regulation losses in that span.

"It was tough to play," Seabrook explains, recalling the beginning of his Chicago tenure. "We were in a dogfight every night and we didn't make the playoffs. It was always tough to be going home in April and watching the other teams in the playoffs."

Obviously, Seabrook has seen a vast improvement with talented additions to every facet of the team, and he sees promise for the future.

"We want to succeed and we want to make the playoffs," he says. "I think we are a good bit younger than we have been in a while. It's a fun group to be around and we're all enjoying what we're doing."

When Seabrook chronicles the seasons to come, hopefully it will end with the success he's only been able to watch from afar. ●

Brent Seabrook tied linemate Duncan Keith for the team lead in points by a defenseman last season (32), while finishing second to Keith in plus/minus (+13).

The 14th-overall pick by the Blackhawks in 2003, Seabrook has made a name for himself with his physical play and offensive ability.

The Four Categories of Everyday Blues

➤ Do you feel unhappy every time you look in the mirror? (If so, you may have the Body-Image Blues.)

➤ Do you feel mad and sad about getting older? (If so, you may have the Age-Rage Blues.)

➤ Are you having trouble juggling your work and home life? (If so, you may have the Working-Parents Blues.)

➤ Do you wonder who that stranger is climbing into bed with you every night? (If so, you may have the Bedroom Blues.)

➤ Are there days when you'd just rather pull the covers over your head than face the day? (If so, you may have the Monday-Morning Blues.)

Everybody gets the blues sometimes—those sad, disheartening, ho-hum feelings we get that make us feel lethargic, sluggish, and bored. There are four general categories for the everyday blues. They include: Relationship blues, Work Blues, Body blues, and Culture blues. Each category has four types of blues that we all get at least some times in our lives.

Relationship Blues

➤ Home-Alone Blues
➤ Bedroom Blues

➤ Pooped-Parent Blues
➤ Parent Approval Blues

Work Blues

➤ Monday-Morning Blues
➤ Bad-Boss Blues

➤ Burnout Blues
➤ Working-Parents Blues

Body Blues

➤ Body-Image Blues
➤ Age-Rage Blues

➤ Cancer Blues
➤ Cardiovascular Blues

Culture Blues

For men:

➤ Decoronation Blues
➤ Age-Rage Blues

For women:

➤ My Fair Lady Blues
➤ Seasonal Blues

alpha
books

Relationship Blues

➤ To beat the Bedroom Blues, learn to communicate your needs and feelings more effectively with your spouse, be aware of the differences in how men and women handle stress, and take the time to rekindle the romance in your relationship.

➤ To better cope with your parents, challenge the rules you were raised with and learn to think and be on your own. You'll also get along better with your parents if you stop trying to convince them that you are right and if you listen to what they have to say without judgment.

➤ The best way to overcome the Pooped-Parent Blues is to practice good discipline, understand your child's temperament, and rate your own amount of burnout—then take corrective action.

➤ Singles can beat the Home-Alone Blues by learning skills to develop and maintain relationships and by accepting the reality that they will have to work hard to make a relationship.

Work Blues

➤ If you have the Burnout Blues, take more control over your time. Make a contract with yourself to organize one area of your life and reward yourself when you've succeeded.

➤ To beat the Monday-Morning Blues, follow your passion and identify the skills you'll need to develop to get a job you'll love.

➤ When you find yourself locked in battle with your boss, stop and think "What have I done to contribute to this?" and accept responsibility for your share of the problem. Then learn to communicate effectively with your supervisor by being a problem solver, not a victim.

➤ To better balance work and family life, find a job that has "family-friendly" policies, get better organized at home so you know where things are, plan ahead so you can save time, and volunteer at your child's school to keep in touch with his or her world.

Body Blues

➤ Make a list of all the negative phrases you've heard about your appearance and write down positive statements next to them. Each time you say to yourself "I look ugly," say instead "I like the way I look, and I have a nice smile."

➤ When you are recovering from heart surgery or an illness, do everything you can to fight negative thinking and stay proactive by assuming control over even the smallest things.

➤ When coping with cancer or other illnesses, learn the three major relaxation techniques and figure out a way you and your family can work with the medical system and alternative medicines to effectively battle your illness.

➤ When food cravings hit, wait 4–12 minutes to see if they pass, or distract yourself with a walk or other activity.

Culture Blues

➤ For men: Learn to identify when you are having an emotional reaction by paying more attention to various physical symptoms like tightness in the throat or chest and back aches.

➤ When you feel down about getting older, lay the groundwork for your future by asking yourself questions about your hopes, responsibilities, and aspirations. Then take steps toward turning two of those hopes into goals.

➤ For women: Write down which traditions brought about by your cultural conscience help you, and look at these good qualities whenever you feel down—then ditch the traditions that stand in your way of progress.

➤ Take control over your feelings by making a list of the conflicts you feel when your cultural conscience bumps up against pressures of daily life so you can see when you get down on yourself and why.

Patrick Sharp

#	Player	Height	Weight	DOB	Age	Birthplace
10	Patrick Sharp "A"	6' 1"	197	Dec 27, 1981	26	Thunder Bay, ON, CAN

Not all investments are blue-chip stocks; there are only so many No. 1 overall draft choices in the NHL. Somewhere along the line, a long-shot investment is going to pay off. If investing in Patrick Sharp three years ago was a risk, he's yielded a healthy reward since then.

"I think my success goes hand-in-hand with the Blackhawks' success," Sharp says. "They've given me a great

opportunity to play since I've been here. I've had good coaches and good teammates. It might surprise some people—the individual success I've had over the past couple of years—but the people in the Hawks organization, I think, could see it coming."

Some 94 players were selected before Sharp was chosen by Philadelphia in the 2001 NHL Entry Draft. The Flyers only gave Sharp 66 games before trading him to Chicago. In his 210 games since then, Sharp has tallied 65 goals and 55 assists, led the 2007–08 Hawks in overall and game-winning goals, and become one of the most reliable scorers on the Blackhawks.

So far this season Sharp is delivering for the team again, moving back to center even though he played all of the previous year on the wing and had the most productive season of his career.

"There are things I need to improve on and focus on, but the team's been winning and the lineup's been working," says Sharp. "There are no complaints on my end, that's for sure."

Sharp has also taken on the leadership role of alternate captain for the season.

"I haven't changed too much. I just try to prepare myself to play hard every night," he says. "I lead by example on the ice and I like to think I take care of myself and my teammates off the ice."

Clearly, Sharp's a stock that just keeps rising. ●

One of its best offensive players and team leaders, the Blackhawks coaching staff named Patrick Sharp an alternate captain for the 2008–09 season.

BLACKHAWK
RADIO NETWORK
670 AM

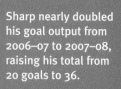

Sharp nearly doubled
his goal output from
2006–07 to 2007–08,
raising his total from
20 goals to 36.

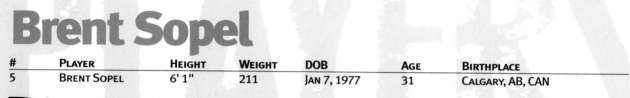

Brent Sopel

#	PLAYER	HEIGHT	WEIGHT	DOB	AGE	BIRTHPLACE
5	BRENT SOPEL	6' 1"	211	JAN 7, 1977	31	CALGARY, AB, CAN

Defenseman Brent Sopel has seen it all. In his 13 years in professional hockey, he's worked his way to the NHL, rebounded from injuries, and played on Stanley Cup contenders. At the age of 31 and still in the prime of his career, Sopel is the oldest skater on the team.

"It's a long season and we have a lot of young guys who haven't been through it," says Sopel. "There are always

questions that need to be asked and things that need to be said. As an older guy, I've been through a lot and played in a lot of playoff games. Sometimes I feel I have to step up and say something."

For the "senior citizen" of the blue line, Sopel has already made a statement during his Blackhawks tenure. After signing a free-agent contract with the Hawks at the start of the 2007–08 season, Sopel appeared in 58 games for the Hawks, tallied 20 points, and had a plus/minus of +9 for the season, earning him a three-year contract extension. This year, he's part of a revamped blue line that features standouts such as Duncan Keith, Brent Seabrook, and newcomer Brian Campbell.

"There are different players here than were here last year and different coaches as well, so there are definitely a lot of differences from last year," says Sopel. "Some things are really different, but defensive systems are similar."

For a player who has seen it all, there's one thing left on his to-do list: win a championship.

"We've got a great bunch of guys in this locker room who know how to win and want to win," he says. "You've got to want to do what it takes every single night, and that ability is definitely in this room." ●

With 10 years NHL experience, Brent Sopel provides the team with veteran leadership on the blue line and inside the locker room.

In 2007–08, his first season with the Hawks, Sopel (shown here between Jonathan Toews and goaltender Cristobal Huet) provided solid defense, posting a plus/minus of +9.

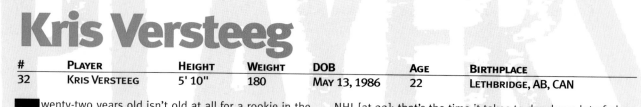

Kris Versteeg

#	PLAYER	HEIGHT	WEIGHT	DOB	AGE	BIRTHPLACE
32	KRIS VERSTEEG	5' 10"	180	MAY 13, 1986	22	LETHBRIDGE, AB, CAN

Twenty-two years old isn't old at all for a rookie in the NHL. That is, unless you're a rookie in the Blackhawks' locker room; if you're 22 there, then you're ancient. Blackhawks players who come to the NHL young, including Patrick Kane, Jonathan Toews, and Brent Seabrook, have wrecked the curve for players such as forward Kris Versteeg.

"It's not a big deal to not have a lot of experience in the NHL [at 22]; that's the time it takes to develop a lot of players," says Versteeg, who had 13 games of NHL experience coming into this season. "We have players around here who you might call 'young phenoms.' They're pretty unbelievable at what they do, but you see a lot more guys coming up at 21 or 22 than you do at 18 or 19."

Versteeg has fought hard for everything he has achieved so far. A former Boston Bruins prospect, he ranked fourth on the Hawks' AHL affiliate, the Rockford IceHogs, in points in 2007–08 (49 in just 56 games).

"A lot of my progress has really been in the mental game," Versteeg says. "I always felt I could play in the NHL; you have to believe you can play in the NHL if you're going to make it. I knew I had the skills, but it's putting all of those things together on a nightly basis." ●

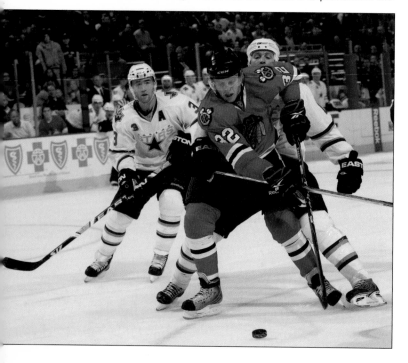

With just 13 NHL games to his credit coming into this season, Kris Versteeg has been one of the biggest surprises thus far in 2008–09.

James Wisniewski

#	PLAYER	HEIGHT	WEIGHT	DOB	AGE	BIRTHPLACE
43	JAMES WISNIEWSKI	6' 0"	207	FEB 21, 1984	24	CANTON, MI, USA

Hockey players become hockey players for a lot of different reasons. Some play the game simply for the love of it. Defenseman James Wisniewski became a hockey player—and one of the fiercest players on the Hawks—for a much different reason.

"I think it's from my sisters beating me up when I was a kid," he says. "I had two older sisters, who were four and six years older, and girls are worse than a lot of the players I face because they never stop. Guys will say 'okay, he's had enough', but my sisters always got in a couple of extra shots. That had a lot to do with it."

Wisniewski has made a name for himself on the Hawks' blue line by being one of the toughest players on the ice, as well as a skilled defender. In 68 games in 2007–08, Wisniewski's plus/minus was the third best among Hawks defenders (+12), and he was second on the team with 103 penalty minutes.

"I just keep thinking 'never quit,'" says Wisniewski. "I just keep on going. You'll have to kill me to stop me."

Wisniewski's mettle has been tested consistently throughout his career; he's been sidelined with a torn ACL three different times, and began the 2008–09 season on injured reserve.

"The toughest part is the mental aspect of going through my third knee surgery," says Wisniewski. "I can almost do the rehabilitation by myself. I just look at this as another stepping stone. I've come back from my other two healthy and ready to play. It's just another speed bump in my career." ●

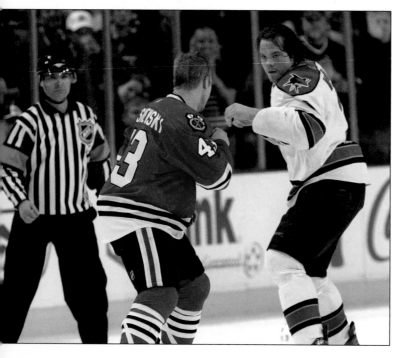

James Wisniewski ranked third among team blueliners with seven goals and 26 points and tied for third with 19 assists in an NHL-career-high 68 matchups last season.

Hawks To Watch

Craig Adams, RW

#	PLAYER	HEIGHT	WEIGHT	DOB	AGE	BIRTHPLACE
28	CRAIG ADAMS	6' 0"	197	APRIL 26, 1977	31	SERIA, BRN

Troy Brouwer, RW

#	PLAYER	HEIGHT	WEIGHT	DOB	AGE	BIRTHPLACE
22	TROY BROUWER	6' 2"	213	AUG 17, 1985	23	VANCOUVER, BC, CAN

Ben Eager, LW

#	PLAYER	HEIGHT	WEIGHT	DOB	AGE	BIRTHPLACE
55	BEN EAGER	6' 2"	220	JAN 22, 1984	24	OTTAWA, ON, CAN

Colin Fraser, C

#	PLAYER	HEIGHT	WEIGHT	DOB	AGE	BIRTHPLACE
46	COLIN FRASER	6' 1"	188	JAN 28, 1985	23	SICAMOUS, BC, CAN

Aaron Johnson, D

#	PLAYER	HEIGHT	WEIGHT	DOB	AGE	BIRTHPLACE
23	AARON JOHNSON	6' 1"	211	APRIL 30, 1983	25	PORT HAWKESBURY, NS, CAN

Matt Walker, D

#	PLAYER	HEIGHT	WEIGHT	DOB	AGE	BIRTHPLACE
8	MATT WALKER	6' 3"	214	APRIL 7, 1980	28	BEAVERLODGE, AB, CAN

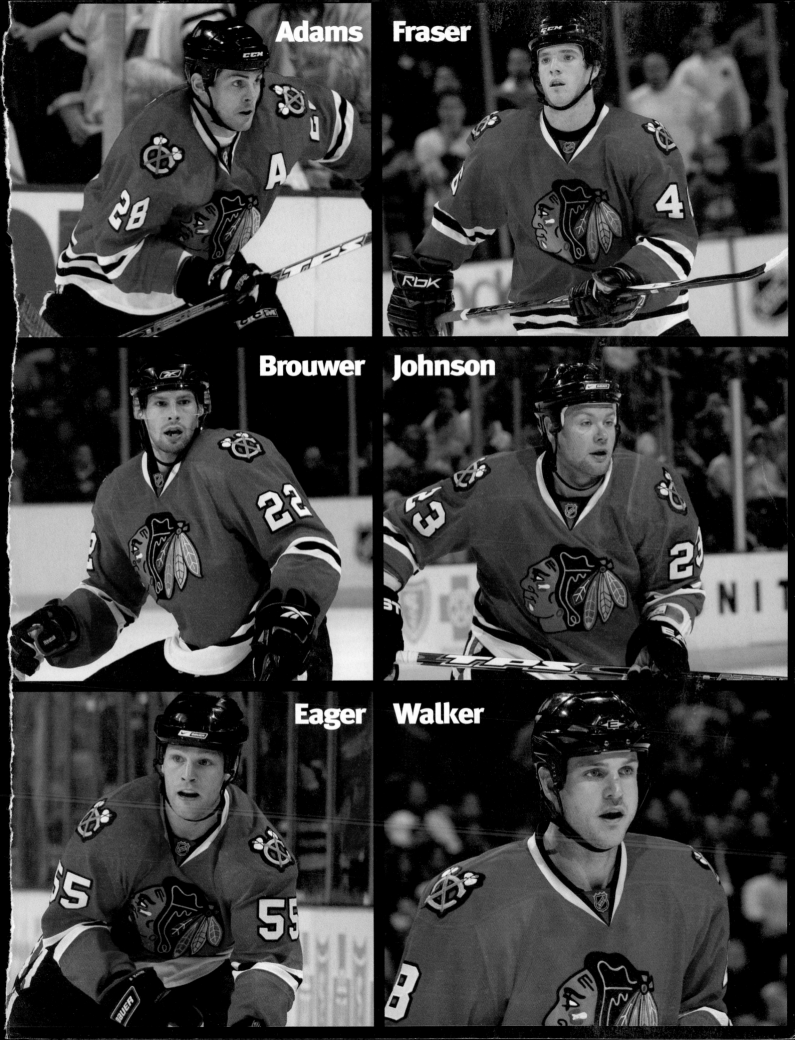

Career Points Leaders

	Player	Pos	From	To	GP	G	A	P	+/-	PIM	PP	SH	GW	GT	Shots
1	Stanley Mikita	C	1958-1959	1979-1980	1,394	541	926	1,467		1,270					
2	Robert Hull	L	1957-1958	1971-1972	1,036	604	549	1,153		640					
3	Denis Savard	C	1980-1981	1996-1997	881	377	719	1,096	98	1,005	101	15	46	3	2,446
4	Stephen Larmer	R	1980-1981	1992-1993	891	406	517	923	182	475	153	19	49	1	2,541
5	Douglas Wilson	D	1977-1978	1990-1991	938	225	554	779	119	764	80	9	23	1	3,060
6	Dennis Hull	L	1964-1965	1976-1977	904	298	342	640		255					
7	Pit Martin	C	1967-1968	1977-1978	740	243	384	627	156	439	51	7	34		1,555
8	Jeremy Roenick	C	1988-1989	1995-1996	524	267	329	596	117	570	108	19	38	7	1,453
9	Anthony Amonte	R	1993-1994	2001-2002	627	268	273	541	67	468	68	20	34	5	1,903
10	Bill Mosienko	R	1941-1942	1954-1955	711	258	282	540		121					
11	Kenny Wharram	R	1951-1952	1968-1969	766	252	281	533		222					
12	Doug Bentley	L	1939-1940	1951-1952	546	217	314	531		215					
13	Robert Murray	D	1975-1976	1989-1990	1,008	132	382	514	20	873	48	3	11	1	2,076
14	Eric Nesterenko	R	1956-1957	1971-1972	1,013	207	288	495		1,012					
15	Troy Murray	C	1981-1982	1993-1994	688	197	291	488	63	707	36	17	29	2	1,239
16	Chris Chelios	D	1990-1991	1998-1999	664	92	395	487	120	1,495	37	7	13	2	1,891
17	Pierre Pilote	D	1955-1956	1967-1968	821	77	400	477		1,205					
18	Clifford Koroll	R	1969-1970	1979-1980	814	208	254	462	109	376	53	5	39		1,458
19	Jim Pappin	R	1968-1969	1974-1975	488	216	228	444	85	447	42	6	35		1,124
20	Chico Maki	R	1960-1961	1975-1976	841	143	292	435		345					
21	Alexei Zhamnov	C	1996-1997	2003-2004	528	140	284	424	19	419	37	8	22	2	1,295
22	Thomas Lysiak	C	1978-1979	1985-1986	474	137	275	412	-40	238	38	5	24		926
23	Eric Daze	L	1994-1995	2005-2006	601	226	172	398	8	176	62	1	34	8	1,607
24	Bill Hay	C	1959-1960	1966-1967	506	113	273	386		244					
25	Mush March	R	1928-1929	1944-1945	759	153	230	383		540					
26	Alan Secord	L	1980-1981	1989-1990	466	213	159	372	13	1,426	62	0	25	0	1,167
27	Johnny Gottselig	L	1928-1929	1944-1945	589	176	195	371		203					
28	Ed Litzenberger	C	1954-1955	1960-1961	438	145	199	344		241					
29	Dirk Graham	R	1987-1988	1994-1995	546	152	191	343	35	628	25	26	26	2	1,292
30	Ivan Boldirev	C	1974-1975	1978-1979	384	140	195	335	-37	186	35	0	15		971